THE
MOTHER~DAUGHTER
BOOK CLUB

HOW TEN BUSY MOTHERS AND DAUGHTERS CAME TOGETHER TO TALK, LAUGH AND LEARN THROUGH THEIR LOVE OF READING

by Shireen Dodson
with Teresa Barker

A Seth Godin Production

HarperPerennial
A Division of HarperCollins*Publishers*

HarperCollins books may be purchased for educational, business, or sales promotional use. For information please write: Special Markets Department, HarperCollins Publishers, Inc., 10 East 53rd Street, New York, NY 10022.

Designed by Susan Brown & Associates

FIRST EDITION

Library of Congress Cataloging-in-Publication Data

Dodson, Shireen.
    The mother-daughter book club / by Shireen Dodson with Teresa Baker.
        p.   cm.
    "A Seth Godin production."
    Includes bibliographical references and index.
    ISBN 0-06-095242-3
    1. Group reading.   2. Mothers and daughters.   3. Mother—Books and reading.   4. Daughters—Books and reading.   I. Baker, Teresa.   II. Title.
LC6619.D63   1997
372.41'62—dc21   97-3702

97 98 99 00 01 HC 10 9 8 7 6 5 4 3 2

To my daughter and my friend, Morgan,
who was the inspiration for it all;
to my husband, Leroy,
who is always there for me;
to my other children,
Leroy III and Skylar, for their love;
and last (but first!), giving honor to God,
who makes all things possible.

CONTENTS

THE MOTHER-DAUGHTER BOOK CLUB
1996

Cheryl Brown and Ashley (age twelve)

Linda Chastang and Rebecca (age eleven)

Alexis Christian and Jamexis (age twelve)

Shireen Dodson and Morgan Fykes (age eleven)

Winnie Donaldson and Tiffany (age eleven)

Leslye Fraser and Brittney (age ten)

Grace Speights and Ashley (age ten)

Alice Lacey Thomas and Holly (age ten)

Kathie Thompson and Jihan (age twelve)

Joyce Yette and Maya (age nine)

INTRODUCTION

Everyone needs to take time off and spend time away. You need that special place where you can cleanse your mind and renew your soul. For me that time is our annual family vacation and the place is Martha's Vineyard. We try to go for at least two weeks in August, and often we can squeeze in three weeks. Not only do I use the time to search inside myself, but I also have a chance to reconnect with my three children, Leroy III, Morgan and Skylar. We talk: We review the past school year and then look ahead. How are they looking at the world around them, and what are they thinking about the year ahead? It is surprising what emerges from your children when you slow down from the hustle and bustle of the usual school and extracurricular routines, step back, look and listen. I am amazed at how much we can discuss in the absence of normal everyday interruptions. At the end of each August, I am always a little bit sad as we drive home to be leaving behind the opportunity to relate to my children in such a relaxed way. Our vacations create a haven for positive interaction to occur spontaneously. I think I was unconsciously trying to figure out a way to carry that feeling back into our regular lives.

During our 1995 summer vacation my morning routine included a walk with a new friend and her daughter along the water's edge. There was something so beautiful and calming about the ocean that conversation just seemed to flow. My friend and I walked and the girls roller-bladed on an adjacent path, which gave us a chance for private conversation. Our talk often turned to our daughters and an only half-joking question: How were we ever going to survive their growing up? After all, children do not come with an instruction manual. And since there is something unique about the mother-daughter relationship, especially as girls approach adolescence, directions of some kind would surely be useful.

So these walks with my friend were comforting confirmation that I was not alone in my difficulty understanding my daughter. Morgan is my middle child, and while she is beautiful, bright and normally very self-confident, she can be vulnerable and moody. In taking stock that summer, I realized that I often mistook Morgan's self-confidence and intellect for maturity, and would sometimes forget that she was only nine. We would argue over every little issue and did not really talk. That's not exactly accurate. We talked a lot. The problem was that we were not communicating. We talked at each other, and while neither of us particularly enjoyed this ongoing power struggle, we didn't know how to change our way of relating. My friend was engaged in a very similar prickly relationship and though the individual skirmishes were different, the struggle was the same.

Like many women I know, I think things through by talking about them. One morning my friend and I were brainstorming aloud about how she could communicate more effectively with her daughter. I was asking all kinds of questions about what she and her daughter liked and didn't like to do. I thought an activity and conversation might flow from some common interest.

Neither of them was into sports, and both had very busy schedules. But they both liked to read. Suddenly I heard myself saying, "Why don't you start a mother-daughter book club?" An idea was born! My friend was intrigued, so I continued to talk it through as we completed our walk. Eventually our conversation moved on to other things, and soon the vacation itself came to an end.

I did, however, mention the idea to my husband, Leroy, on the drive home. This time, when I heard myself talking about a mother-daughter book club, I thought of Morgan and me. Morgan and I both love to read. As the previous discussion with my friend flooded back into my mind I realized that all the comments about her and her daughter also applied to Morgan and me. I made up my mind right then to start a book club—and soon. I felt a sense of wonder and hope for the upcoming year. Our experience has been gratifying and continues to be.

Yes, Morgan and I still have an occasional fight, but the atmosphere at home is much improved. We no longer have to wait for August and Martha's Vineyard to find a peaceful haven. The

Mother-Daughter Book Club offers us that kind of harmony all through the year.

Just as we occasionally invite guests to our Mother-Daughter Book Club meetings, it seemed natural to invite guests into our book to share their wisdom on the subject of literature and the lives of girls and women. They joined us enthusiastically. These authors, educators, counselors and others, through interviews or letters, contributed an abundance of practical tips, candid advice, personal memories and suggestions for reading, all of which are here for you to savor.

With this book in hand, then, welcome to a very special meeting of the Mother-Daughter Book Club.

SHIREEN DODSON
December 1996

CHAPTER ONE

WHY START A MOTHER~DAUGHTER BOOK CLUB?

To our mothers and grandmothers, aunts and great-aunts.

To all the women who stood before us, telling us about where they came

from, what they saw, did and imagined. They let us know they stood

for us. Talking, they combed our hair, rocked us to sleep, sang to us,

told us tales of then and now—and tomorrow. They worried about us.

They hoped for us and showed us the way. They cared.

—VIRGINIA HAMILTON, *dedication,* Her Stories

Hello. My name is Morgan Fykes. I'm eleven years old and I live in a large, old house with a big porch and a room of my own in Washington, D.C. I'm in fifth grade at National Cathedral School for Girls, along with five of the other girls in our club—Jamexis, Ashley S., Jihan, Rebecca and Tiffany.

I'm cheerful and I talk a lot, except when I'm meeting new people and I don't know what they like to talk about.

One thing I enjoy is reading. That's one reason I love our book club so much. The other good things about it are that I get to play and talk more with my friends and I get to be with my mom and hear her ideas when they aren't about cleaning up my room or doing my homework. I also like art—I have an art section set up in one corner of my basement— and dancing (tap, ballet and jazz), sports, swimming and camping.

I'm a Girl Scout and we go on lots of camping trips. My Girl Scout troop went to Savannah and visited the Juliette Lowe house. We saw her room—I even got to put on some old-fashioned clothes with stays. Those were really uncomfortable!

My mom is Shireen Dodson—Dodson because she kept her maiden name, and that's fine with me and my dad. This whole Mother-Daughter Book Club was her idea. She's sort of the leader of the club, but for her real job she is the assistant director at the Smithsonian Institution's Center for African American History and Culture. That's a good job for her, since she says she's a "pack rat"—like me—and likes to collect things for a hobby. She collects African American Christmas ornaments, which is very nice for our whole family. I have a sixteen-year-old brother named Leroy—like my father—and a six-year-old sister named Skylar.

I read a lot of books in series, like the Boxcar Children and the Baby-sitters Club. My favorite book from the club so far has been *The Ear, the Eye, and the Arm,* by Nancy Farmer.

What mother doesn't have a secret agenda, that designing hope in our hearts when we plot good times for our children? The family vacations, the slumber parties, the diary, the model horses. Sometimes we yearn to give them what we didn't have at their age. Sometimes it's an ember of memory we hope to fan into a glow to warm their lives. Either way, no matter what we had in mind when we planned it, the reality always holds some surprises.

When I first thought of organizing the Mother-Daughter Book Club, I'll admit I had an agenda. I had a plan. I was motivated. But it wasn't memories that moved me, although I had some good ones. And it wasn't as if I had some soulful longing for literary discussion, though I've always enjoyed the company of women and girls. No, my motivation was planted very firmly in the here and now.

My daughter Morgan had just turned nine years old, and we enjoyed the full range of emotions and dialogue you might expect of two creative, determined females with a generation between them. It seemed like we were constantly butting heads over everyday things. More and more, I realized that I needed

"I spend time with each of my children, one-on-one, but I like the Mother-Daughter Book Club because it is not just you and the child, but a group of peers and parents all having something in common. And all of us are interested in wanting to build more of a relationship between mother and daughter."

ALICE

—and wanted—to find a way to spend some special time with Morgan that would help us understand each other better and give us a close relationship as she grew up.

WHAT IS IT ABOUT GIRLS...

Like a lot of other mothers, I was beginning to ask myself: "How do you know what girls are actually thinking about? How do you plant the seeds of the values you want to take hold in their lives if they won't listen to you when you talk to them one-on-one?"

Another mother of a preteen daughter put it this way: "We can be standing on the same square foot of earth, looking up at the same sky, and we still manage to see things differently. We get along fine, but I suspect that when it comes to knowing what she's really thinking about things, the truth is often I don't have a clue."

All of us — mothers and daughters alike — do see things differently. Not only that, we actually *see different things.* It's like what happens at the checkout line at the supermarket when you're waiting there, confronted with tabloids and magazines with headlines that shout about every conceivable angle on life: how to get a man, how to please a man, how to diet, how to dress for success from the boardroom to the bedroom, how to have great sex, how to flatten your stomach, thin your thighs, quit smoking— the headlines go on and on and on. I'm gazing at those covers and not giving them a second thought. I know fact from fiction when it comes to suggestions about my body, my relationships and my life. But when Morgan, or the girl behind us or the one after her, reads those covers, what happens to all those lifestyle messages, those images of flawless supermodels and carousing celebrities? Our girls don't need books to be readers. They're reading the world everywhere they go, from the checkout line to the television. All day our daughters are gathering images and ideas about the world, about themselves and about their futures.

As caring mothers, we want to know what they're making of it. Sometimes we do know. Sometimes we just wish we did, maybe

> *"You always have these great goals of doing something special with your child, and then the laundry comes up. Having the structure of the book club seems like a nice way to spend some time with your daughter and her friends and see what they're thinking about."*
>
> LESLYE

ON READING AND DISCUSSION

It's really good to get children actively reading. Their minds are working all the time, so ask them a question and encourage them to go a bit further.

It's especially meaningful for a girl, because I think in school girls still tend to be a little reticent and hesitate to speak up. In this safe setting, talking about literature with friends and with her mother, the child can learn how to express her ideas and feelings openly. The experience of being listened to is terribly important. If a mother can do that for her daughter, then she is helping her develop the basis for confidence in her own power to think and to look at things.

Sometimes children are locked into their own realities. They can become trapped in their own perceptions. One of the great positive and liberating things about discussing a rich story is seeing all the different ways of looking at it that people in the group bring. It can be highly motivating, a kind of revelation for the child.

Start with their ideas and show that you really value what they have to say, and then gently go beyond the initial response. Ask, "Can you explain that further, show us where you got that idea?" a very gentle but consistent drawing out.

Generally, children really do blossom when they're listened to.

—ALICE LETVIN, PRESIDENT
The Great Books Foundation

with the hope that if we knew what they were thinking we could cheer on the conclusions we like and changed the ones we didn't.

Direct questions don't get you anywhere, either. What does a girl think about the glimpses of life she sees or hears each day in advertising, on television and in popular music? What does she make of it all?

"Nothing," shrugs Morgan, now eleven.

I don't believe that. But I do believe that's precisely what most girls would say if you asked them. They *don't* know what they're making of it. As their mothers, we're finding out the hard way—from our own experiences or those of families around us—that the culture imposes harshly on our girls' views of themselves, of us and of their prospects for the future.

In *Reviving Ophelia: Saving the Selves of Adolescent Girls*, author Mary Pipher, a clinical psychologist, tells us something most of us already know in our hearts:

"In order to keep their true selves and grow into healthy adults, girls need love from family and friends, meaningful work, respect, challenges and physical and psychological safety. They need identities based on talents or interests rather than appearance, popularity or sexuality. They need good habits for coping with stress, self-nurturing skills and a sense of purpose and perspective. They need quiet places and times. They need to feel that they are part of something larger than their own lives and that they are emotionally connected to the whole."

"In the group, I can be the mom, or the professional, or the 'aunt,' if you will, to the other girls—and they get to see various sides of me—we see different sides of each other, and that is good."

ALEXIS

Other formal studies deliver similar conclusions. Despite some differences in cultural attitudes among girls of different races or ethnic groups, one common theme comes through loud and clear: Life circumstances and the messages girls absorb from their world shape their attitudes about themselves and other girls.

So, if our life circumstances include the scream of high-tech audio-video-electronic cultural influences, how can the calm, purposeful pursuit of books and conversation begin to make a significant difference?

WHAT IS IT ABOUT BOOKS...

Books have always been a refuge, a place where we put aside the routine of the day and step into someone else's story, where we can laugh, cry, gasp or wonder at the goings-on without being responsible for any of it. The story's success doesn't depend on our wisdom or patience; the main character isn't waiting for us to drive her to dance class or pick up poster board for a homework assignment.

Books are a great equalizer. You may not have the money to travel the world, but with a library card as your passport your horizons for exploration and self-discovery are unlimited. You can visit cultures from around the globe, and learn about *anything* that interests you.

Reading can be emotionally freeing as well, as one woman shared with me: "I was a very sick child, alone a lot, and books became my friend," she said. "If you come to a sad place in a book, you can cry and the book doesn't tell you to stop. You can laugh, reading a book, when you might not be able to laugh with other people. If you're shy, or sick

> ### BOOKS TO GROW ON
>
> Books of undeserved obscurity, I call them:
>
> *The Mouse and His Child,*
> Russell Hoban
>
> *The Gammage Cup,*
> Carol Kendall
>
> *Drop Dead,*
> Julia Cunningham
>
> *Jingo Django,*
> Sid Fleischman
>
> *Elidor,*
> Stan Garner
>
> *Goody Hall,*
> Natalie Babbitt
>
> —CYNTHIA VOIGT, AUTHOR
> *Homecoming*

MOTHERS AND DAUGHTERS: CREATING A CIRCLE OF CARING, SHARING

I would like to think that the Mother-Daughter Book Club would be a time for mothers to share stories of their own childhood. I look at my own nieces and nephews and I tell them stories, and they look through our family album and they laugh. There is a time perhaps for some sharing to go on.

In *Addy* there's a part about double Dutch jumping rope, you know, and when I'm talking to groups of moms and girls, the jumping rope is something these mothers remember from when they were girls. But a lot of the kids are shocked to learn that their mothers jumped rope—that they learned double Dutch. They kind of look at you as being grown, and a woman, and they never see you were a child, a child with weird hair and weird clothes. And you can say, "I've gone through what you're going through."

There's that age when they start to believe that their lives are drastically different from any other life on the planet and they need to understand that their moms went through the same things.

It's natural to start pulling away at that age—you're forming who you are—and sometimes there needs to be some distance to let you be the woman you're going to become, but if you've formed that bond, you can come back to it. That bond will still be there after all that. My mom is one of my best friends. I can talk with her about anything—men, work, anything.

There's this popular culture thing going on where it's, "I hate my mother." Our girls don't have to get that popular notion.

I was talking to a little girl, and we were talking about extended family. She described extended family as "not someone you were born to, but someone who loves you like they were." I really think that's been a continuing part of many communities, a sense that other people look out for you, care about you. And it's beneficial for everybody, having people who have entered the family that way. That's what's been lost in society today. We need to find ways to bring it back.

— CONNIE PORTER, AUTHOR
The American Girl Collection, Addy series

or just alone, you can experience emotions you couldn't experience any other way."

If you've ever read a book and chatted about it with someone, or enjoyed a lively group discussion, then you know that books can be bridges as well. Book talk fills the gentle open spaces of time and distance between friends. It can span generations, and criss-cross the textured geography of differing cultures. It makes a neat, quick plank for conversation with someone new. You don't have to know someone to talk books with them, but when you talk books with someone, you're getting to know them.

When we share the experience of reading with our children, books create a garden, a special sunlit corner where our relationship can grow alongside but apart from the crowded landscape of everyday life.

That's what the Mother-Daughter Book Club is all about. Staking out that special garden space, tending it lightly together, inviting a handful of others to join in and sharing the harvest of pleasure and discovery. And the growing season never ends!

WHAT IS IT ABOUT LIFE...

Our daughters need this growing space. They are partners with us in family life, but as they grow, so does their excitement at the very prospect of growing up and the independence that comes with it. As they search for their own authentic life view, the voice that comes from their own heart, they're listening to the voices all around them: those of family, friends and teachers, as well as magazine covers, fashion and lifestyle trends, news headlines and the din of popular culture.

At school—no matter how good the program—they make their way in that tangled woods, on a good day exercising their minds and developing their talents as the culture permits. The forest is thick with the undergrowth of social, emotional and developmental issues, and it grows thicker as each year progresses.

Academics? In studies conducted by the American Association of University Women, researchers have described the typical school culture as one that teaches our daughters to silence themselves, discounting their learning styles, curbing their questions and focusing instead upon striving to please.

In short, the confident girl who spoke up with a math answer in September may only occasionally be raising her hand by November and will feign ignorance by December to avoid the brand of "brain."

Even so, the desire for recognition is there and the competition is fierce. Especially as they become increasingly sensitive to boys' reactions, girls may become reluctant to take the intellectual risks—with the potential for failure—that are necessary to build confidence and competence. And the pressure is on whether the girls attend school with boys or with girls only. In their preteen years, girls can become cliquish in the worst ways, imposing social suffering on other girls who differ in any way from the in-group's power brokers that day.

> **BOOKS TO GROW ON**
>
> My first memory is *Go, Dog, Go*, the part about the hat.
> I remember being fascinated by *James and the Giant Peach*.
>
> *James and the Giant Peach*,
> Roald Dahl
>
> *The Borrowers*,
> Mary Norton
>
> *Charlotte's Web*,
> E. B. White
>
> *Go, Dog, Go*,
> Philip D. Eastman
>
> *Little Women*,
> Louisa May Alcott
>
> —JAMIE LEE CURTIS,
> ACTRESS, AUTHOR
> *Tell Me Again About the Night I Was Born*

At the end of a long school day, many girls step out the door and into a rush of after-school classes where they pursue their special interests. We juggle car pool duty or on our own get them where they need to go: dance, soccer, music, swimming, drama, art, gymnastics. If we see them at all, it's to pump them up with a snack, pop them into a car, and, between traffic lights, practice our gentle art of motherly interrogation to learn something, *anything*, about their day:

"What did you learn today?" I'll ask Morgan on the way home from school. Her reply: "I don't know. Stuff."

Direct questions just never get you anywhere.

Evenings are prime time for conversation. But there's housework, homework and other preparation for tomorrow's return to the hubbub of work and school. Fortunately for me, Morgan is a night owl, and we share our reading and chat time at an hour when most of her friends are already asleep. After a typical day, most mothers and daughters we know consider the night a success if they can squeeze in time for a hug and a kiss on the way to sleep.

"When they're on their own and it's girls only, there are different dynamics than in a mixed group with boys. There's a lot more honesty, connecting and sharing."

WHITNEY RANSOME
National Coalition of Girls' Schools

So, how could *another* organized activity—and a group one, at that—be so satisfying and rewarding? I think it's because a mother-daughter book club doesn't *require*, it *invites*. Instead of obligations, it offers enrichment. It takes what we bring to it—a love of reading, lively conversation and friendship—and amplifies those pleasures. The club format provides just enough structure so we can relax. And into the comfortable familiarity of our circle, it introduces with each book a raft of new characters, with their own ideas and experiences, to broaden our view.

WHAT IS IT ABOUT A MOTHER~DAUGHTER BOOK CLUB...

It doesn't matter if you haven't taken time to read a novel in years. Or if your daughter seems to read only when it's assigned at school. Whether or not you or your daughter is a devoted readers, the Mother-Daughter Book Club works because it isn't just about books. And it isn't just about reading or mastering analytical skills. It's about mothers and daughters, girls and women, and how reading and talking together can enrich our relationships with one another and strengthen our daughters' courage to be themselves.

The benefits are real, and we see them in action not only at our meetings, but in the girls' lives at home, at school and all around.

THE CLUB ENCOURAGES READING

The girls read because they want to. The club motivates the girls to read. Some love reading anyway. But others read because they want to be prepared for the discussion and any activities planned around the book.

"They're not all girls who like to read and have great analytical skills, but they all are excited about coming to socialize," says Linda Chastang. "For the girl who doesn't like to read so much, if she wants to come to that meeting, she's going to read that book."

The before-and-after snapshots of our girls as readers provide some convincing evidence:

"Prior to the Mother-Daughter Book Club, Tiffany's only craving for books was Goosebumps," says Winnie Donaldson. "I was glad she was reading anything. But over the past year, the club has encour-

"Maya and her friends were beginning to have more frequent 'whispered conversations.' Reading the same books has helped us to have more in common as she approaches the age when children begin to distance themselves from their parents."

JOYCE

aged her to want to read other books. She's become a more serious reader. It truly is important to her that she reads the book club book so she'll be prepared to participate in discussion at the meetings."

The girls' approach to reading changes and improves, too, we've noticed.

"She's become a very active reader," says Grace Speights, about her daughter, Ashley. "She'll stop and say something like,

'That's stupid,' or 'Why did that character do that?' and she'll ask about similes or metaphors she doesn't understand. She really asks questions. And I can tell she enjoys it because she'll ask, 'Are we going to read tonight?' and she'll be standing there with the book in hand."

CRITICAL THINKING SKILLS
GET A WORKOUT

Through discussions of the plots, characters, and authors' writing styles, the girls are learning how to take an idea and pull it apart to see what makes it tick, build on it, question it, find evidence to support their opinion of it and use that experience to reflect in greater depth on their own lives or the lives of others.

"These kids are really reading these books and connecting things," says Leslye Fraser. "They'll say things like, 'I'd give it an 8.5,' and they'll analyze the good and the bad, and they'll say the author should have done this or that. It's been nice watching them be in charge, assuming the leadership role with no problem, no fear. And they encourage each other."

It seems like we each see a success story unfolding in our daughter's life.

Alice Thomas recalls how impressed she was the first time she heard her daughter Holly hold forth on the book of the day: "I knew she was getting the story okay, but when we got to the meeting and I heard her talking about all these details in the story, and tying them together to make a statement about the character, I was just amazed—I had no idea she was thinking that deeply about it—and I was proud."

These girls, who can't remember to close the door on their way out, nonetheless remember intricate details of plots and characters that pass through our discussion circle:

"I'm always pleasantly surprised at how girls compare characters from book to book, or reflect on different writing styles," says Joyce Yette. "Maybe I should get used to the fact that they're bright and curious, but I wouldn't have imagined these kinds of discussions."

Books to Grow On

This is a list of books from my childhood, which was a long time ago since I am now eighty. Today's children, it seems to me, are missing so much not reading more folk and fairy tales.

English Fairy Tales and *More English Fairy Tales*, Joseph Jacobs

Grimms' Fairy Tales, Jacob and Wilhelm Grimm

Blue Fairy Book and *Red Fairy Book*, Andrew Lang

Heidi, Johanna Spyri

The Secret Garden, Frances Hodgson Burnett

Little Women, Louisa May Alcott

Jane Eyre, Charlotte Brontë

Dandelion Cottage, Carroll Watson Rankin

Downright Dencey, Caroline Dale Snedeker

—BEVERLY CLEARY, AUTHOR

Ramona the Pest

A Friendly Forum for
Discussing Important Issues

By talking about the impersonal—plots, characters and author's choices—we've heard the girls' candid thoughts on important issues like death and illness, friendship and marriage, family relationships and school and social issues.

"What's been nice is gaining some insight into how they think," Leslye says. "We sometimes take for granted that our children share our life experience—for instance, some of the unhappy things we could all remember from our childhoods—but their comments make it clear that those experiences aren't necessarily part of their lives. That has been a pleasant surprise."

"Some of the issues in the books have been a little delicate, but we talk about them anyway," says Alexis Christian. "If we don't talk about it, who else will? Who do we want the girls to talk about sensitive issues with, if not us?"

A Chance to See Friends,
Make Friends Outside School

The smaller group size and the emotional comfort level of a mother-daughter book club makes it a safe, supportive place for a girl to venture outside the lines she draws for herself each day at school. The combination of laughter, play and talk creates a natural habitat for learning within a circle of caring mothers.

"It gives the girls an opportunity to discuss books without being under pressure like they are at school, wondering if this is the answer the teacher is looking for," says Kathie Thompson. "In our book club there are no right or wrong answers. You can say what you feel."

Even the girls who are bit shy, who typically might be reluctant to say what they feel, are finding a voice in our circle.

"This close, supportive setting has provided an excellent opportunity for Maya, who has always been so shy and quiet, to express herself," says her mom, Joyce. "With each meeting, her voice has become a little louder, her eye contact has become a little more direct and her confidence has grown a little stronger."

Morgan likes the speak-up-and-be-heard atmosphere, too. Says she: "It's much easier than school because you're not writing, you're just talking. A lot of the kids in the club like to talk a lot, so it's nice because that's what we're *supposed* to do!"

STRENGTHENS THE MOTHER~DAUGHTER RELATIONSHIP

Relationships are built on understanding, and this is an easy, gentle way to gain understanding. There are very few regular opportunities in our lives to relax and enjoy one another's company and express our feelings or ideas about what goes on in the world without lecturing.

"One thing I like is that we're able to look at things from a different perspective and try to start helping them think from a different perspective," says Cheryl Brown. "Often the way we phrase our questions is deliberately done so we generate some new thoughts. You don't want to provide answers for the girls, but kind of help them see it differently. A mother can rephrase things, pull ideas out and focus on them, and ask some thought-provoking questions."

Whatever our differences in perspective, the time we share talking at meetings and at home brings us closer to our daughters in ways that feel right.

"The relationship between mothers and daughters in those teen years can get a little strained," Alexis says, "but at this stage, it's a wonderful opportunity for me to actually sit down with Jamexis, even a chance to touch her—stroke her hair, make sure she's okay—it's some real time we can share and be best friends because women can become best friends, and hopefully she'll understand she can tell me anything because I plan to tell her everything."

We all share that desire for emotional closeness with our children, and the challenge of creating ways for it to grow.

ABOUT OUR DAUGHTERS:
WORRY LESS, WONDER MORE

When we're trying so hard to be perfect, or we're feeling so pressed for time, or holding up standards for ourselves that are impossible to reach, part of what we ask of our children is that they fit into our plans so we can manage and know them completely, rather than see them as someone we're interested in or curious about in a deeper way. We need to wonder more about what they're thinking and who they are.

I'm not talking about an endless interrogation, but this is a good place where reading stories together can be a really fun way to get to know your daughter in a different way and be open and curious about her and how she thinks.

—ELIZABETH DEBOLD, DEVELOPMENTAL PSYCHOLOGIST
coauthor of Mother Daughter Revolution: From Good Girls to Great Women

"It's difficult, because in the normal flow of the parent-child relationship at this age the parent is viewed as the authoritarian who will be angry or upset if you say something wrong," Grace says. "It's hard for them to cross the line—they're thinking, 'This is my mom, but she's also my friend,' and until you have some kind of relationship where you can show that side in a natural way, it's a hard thing to do. This gives us a chance to do that. I want Ashley to view me as a mom who is open and willing to talk about anything that she wants to talk about, no matter what the subject."

"The funniest thing that happened at a meeting was when we discussed the folk tales in Her Stories *by Virginia Hamilton, and our moms asked us to describe the man that we would like to marry. Although we had all been very talkative at every meeting, this question from the moms just caused us to giggle."*

ASHLEY S.

A WHOLESOME FEELING OF BELONGING

Along with the fun, the group provides affirmation—a feeling of recognition and acceptance—that our adolescent girls need. A story I heard one evening at a Girl Scout board meeting left me and a room full of others in tears, and it tells me we're right to be concerned and we're on the right track with our book discussion club. The speaker told us of a letter she had received from a college girl—a former Girl Scout. The young woman had written that she was sitting at her desk at 3 a.m., her roommate in the throes of an emotional crisis, feelings of despair thick in the dormitory room. She wrote about the emotional tempests of college life, but added that she was keeping an even keel, and concluded that it was her experience as a Girl Scout that had given her a strong, sure belief in herself.

There really are very few places where girls get that message

HOW CAN WE HELP OUR CHILDREN BECOME ENTHUSIASTIC READERS?

On the one hand, you leave them alone, and on the other, you read with them. Don't force books on children. When I was a child, all my reading was done without any kind of organization, and I try to approach reading in a similar way with my daughter. If I really want her to read something, I may just slip it into her room, but seldom more than that. Because if they discover it on their own, it's what they want.

And don't be too worried about what they choose. There are protests from time to time about certain children's books: Parents think they are too cruel, too this, too that. Usually, these are the books that children love most. Children really do want to know how to deal with life; they want those truths. And you have to let them discover a book that gives them a way to incorporate such lessons into life, and that also gives them some pleasure in the hard truth.

The second part of the solution is to read with them. It sounds so corny, but it's true: If you make that time to sit down and read them something, and not just when they are little and can't read, but when they are older and can read, and you read together, it makes all the difference in the world.

Eventually, they will get to the point where they think it's uncool to do that. Then you find something that's really funny, and you read it aloud in parts. Or, when you find that they don't want you to read something to them, then you just read it, too. So you say: "We're going to read this book: You read it, and I'm going to read it, and then we can talk about it." Now of course, when you talk about it, you don't do it in any kind of quiz way, you just talk about it. I've found that this really works.

For instance, my daughter is now falling into the *Star Trek* age, and she is reading some of those books, and they are horrible books. But I'm reading the *Star Trek* books, too, because then I can talk to her about them. And when we talk about those, then we can also talk about *Sophie's World* and the other good books, which she also reads. I try not to convey any sense that I'm too good to talk about those other books. And if I feel tempted, as I sometimes do, to say something like: "You know, these are really terrible books," I remember my comic books and *Mad* magazine, and I bite my lip.

—RITA DOVE
U.S. Poet Laureate

of affirmation in a continuing way. Our Mother-Daughter Book Club does that for our daughters.

The Mother-Daughter Book Club provides a kind of balance to the life our girls experience at school and the view they see of mothers at home or at work. They even experience *each other* differently than they do in other settings.

"We don't all go to the same school and see each other every day, so when we get together, it's like a party, and you play and play until it's time to go home," says Holly Thomas, ten. "The book discussion is fun, so it's like part of the party."

"It's really nice if you like reading *and* if you want to make more friends *and* if you want to get to know people better," says Maya Yette, ten. "It's fun to get to play at other people's houses more."

"It gives you the chance to talk about the books so you're not just reading them and putting them down. You're really understanding."

MAYA

Those simple thoughts ring true. Even the girls who knew one another well have seen their relationships flower around our meeting discussions.

"My favorite part of the book club meetings is the social part, when we eat and talk and play games," says Rebecca Chastang, eleven. "The books are okay, too."

Our reading, meetings and discussion allow our girls the freedom to focus on:

★ **Sharing instead of competition:** There's eagerness in the discussion but never a race to see who can "win" the race to give a right answer. "In school, there's always a right and wrong answer, so usually I don't answer if I think I might get it wrong," says Brittney Fraser, ten. "This was new to me—I was nervous at first because I thought everybody was going to say 'No!' like they do in class. But they didn't."

★ **Reflection instead of performance:** By posing questions that draw on the girls' experience as well as their understanding of a story, the discussion invites thought and comment. It encourages reflection, because the more thought you put into an answer, the more everyone responds to it, and that's an immediate source of enjoyment for everyone. "When we read the book *The Friends* by Rosa Guy, I liked that book," says Ashley Brown, twelve. "The fact that it talks about friendship and how there are problems sometimes, but you can work things out. It made me think about my friends."

★ Acceptance instead of judgment: Discussion offers a safe haven for expression. Since every perspective is valuable in an open discussion, each person's comments receive the same respect and acknowledgment. Some comments lead to more vigorous discussion than others, but it's not because the comment is good or bad. It's the chemistry of the moment, and the girls quickly become comfortable in that judgment-free zone. "I never knew it was so easy to express your opinions," says Ashley Speights, ten. "I used to be very shy about that, but now it doesn't seem so hard to say what I think about something."

★ Exploration instead of mastery: The shy one can speak without fear of ridicule, and the perfectionist learns to share her full rainbow of ideas instead of narrowing her contributions to just "the right answer." The careful exploration of ideas helps girls develop a sense of mastery, a comfort level with critical thinking skills that they need to hold their own in other circles or circumstances. "When we're all talking about the same book, some people have different ideas and it opens up a new perspective you didn't even think about, and then you listen and understand it," says Jamexis Christian, twelve.

★ Experience instead of objectives: In most other realms of our lives we face a constant pressure to achieve results: meet deadlines, make good grades, meet expectations of our own or of others. You can't make an A in the Mother-Daughter Book Club; there is no performance review. The experience is what there is, all there is, and it is the experience that teaches us the most about the books and about ourselves. "Discussing the book is my favorite part of the meeting," says Jihan Thompson, twelve. "Sometimes the mothers might bring up a topic, and people will say how they feel about it or give their views on the book. It's really fun to get different people's insights on it."

★ **Seeing mothers as individuals instead of experts or managers:** Mothers enjoy the same respectful treatment as every member of the discussion group, and that sense of equality in this setting allows our girls to see us more as individuals, as interesting women with thoughts to share. Here, our years of life experience don't make us "boss." Our experience only adds to the richness of the conversation.

It didn't take Morgan long to warm up to some real conversation. "At our very first meeting, some of us weren't so used to doing things like this with our moms, but once we got started talking, it just started flowing and then it was just great," Morgan says. "Now it's always that way."

The fact that we're all so busy, mothers and daughters alike, makes it a special experience when we simply sit down in a place together to talk—instead of *to get something done.*

"I have homework, and she has work and Girl Scouts," says Tiffany Donaldson, eleven, whose mother, Winnie, is a Girl Scout leader, among other things. "When I'm home, I'm reading or working on homework and she's doing Girl Scouts and other stuff, so I pretty much don't get to talk to her. I like hearing her ideas about our books at the meetings."

What's in it for us, the mothers? Some of the benefits are those we had in mind when we started—dreams come true:

★ We express ourselves as individuals, beyond our roles in the family, community or workplace.

★ We treasure this special time with our daughters outside the flurry of family life.

Books to Grow On

Some of these came from my "Women Writing in French" course. Others came from my work on women and girls and general reading.

So Long a Letter, Mariama Ba

Mother to Daughter, Daughter to Mother, edited by Tillie Olsen

Meeting at the Crossroads: Women's Psychology and Girls' Development,
Lyn Mikel Brown and Carol Gilligan

The Book of the City of Ladies, Christine de Pizan

The Lais of Marie de France, Marie de France

Women's Friendships: A Collection of Short Stories,
edited by Susan Koppelman

Between Mothers and Daughters: Stories Across a Generation,
edited by Susan Koppelman

—ELLEN SILBER
Director of the Marymount Institute for the Education of Women and Girls

✷ We enjoy the company of women and girls with a similar interest in exploring literature and the world of ideas and intellectual exchange. "As we explore places we probably will never visit, talk about things that probably would not come up in the ordinary course of our lives, get to know characters unlike any we'd ever meet and share our thoughts and experiences with other mothers and their daughters," Linda says, "we have grown closer and we have learned a lot about each other—how alike and different we are, and how much we learn from each other."

Beyond those gifts was a surprise that I never anticipated that day I took my quiet agenda of hope and put it into action: the experience of discovering *myself*, the *woman* at the heart of the mother, daughter, wife, sister, colleague and friend that I am to others. Through reading and chatting with Morgan, and exploring our stories together with the women and girls in our group, it's as if we're picking up our threads of experience, some old, some new, and weaving them into the fabric of our lives today. It is a comfortable cloth, with texture and color, and it has the feel of truth.

A mother-daughter book club gives you and your daughter the space in your relationship and your schedules to do all this, and you don't have to be an "expert" to make it happen. You don't need a college degree in literature, and your daughter doesn't have to get A's in reading at school to enjoy a mother-daughter book club. You've already got all you need: a desire to spend some quality time with your daughter and a willingness to do something about it!

MOTHER-DAUGHTER BOOK CLUB:
OPEN MINDS, OPEN VOICES

Look at a group of eleven-, twelve-, thirteen-year-old girls—it's a hoot! They laugh, they're spontaneous, they're joyful, they're loving, they take pleasure in a wide variety of things. Girls go through a critical passage from age eleven to fourteen—fifth grade through ninth grade. They begin with a tremendous amount of interest and enthusiasm, pleasure in the things around them and themselves.

Then as they start to make the transition between girlhood and young womanhood, it's like walking through a minefield, in terms of the images before them about how they should look, how they should act, what they wear, what they think, what they do. All of that begins to narrow and limit how they perceive themselves. They don't start out that way. It's our job to help them keep that spontaneity.

— WHITNEY RANSOME
Coexecutive Director, National Coalition of Girls' Schools

ENDNOTES

* Literature and discussion can strengthen the bond between mothers and daughters.

* A mother-daughter book club encourages reading.

* The reading club format gives girls a chance to develop critical thinking skills outside the classroom.

* An intimate circle of mothers, daughters and friends provides a sense of affirmation and a place to be heard.

CHAPTER TWO

HOW TO ORGANIZE YOUR BOOK CLUB

The reading and discussion group is as enduring

as the written word, for as long as words have been written,

people have read, contemplated and gathered

to talk about them.

— ALAN MOORES, RHEA RUBIN

"Let's Talk About It," American Library Association

ASHLEY & CHERYL BROWN

Hi, my name is Ashley. I'm twelve years old and I'm in the sixth grade. I like to dance and sing and hang out with my friends. I've taken dance lessons since I was three years old and really love that a lot. I'm artistic, too, and I like to write plays and stories. I'm not really shy, but sometimes I think for a minute before answering questions so I may not be the first one talking.

Sometimes at home, when I'm not writing I'll play with my brother or watch TV. Sometimes, when I hang out with friends, we'll go shopping. That means we go to the mall and try on clothes, then we come back and tell our parents what we want and ask them if we can buy it, and then my mom and I will go back again if I can buy it.

I enjoy pets, dogs the most, but we don't have one. My mom had a dog when she was young and it kept biting her shoes! I like birds, too, and I see them when I visit my friends.

My mom's name is Cheryl and she's a counselor at an elementary school and she's very nice and very caring. She's also very smart. I go to her when I have a problem and she helps me solve it. She's also playful— she plays with my brother and me and jokes a lot and makes me laugh, and then I end up joking, too. She's my really good friend.

My favorite book from the club was *The Friends*, by Rosa Guy. I liked that book because it was about friendship and how sometimes there are problems between friends and you can work things out. I liked it and it made me think about my friends.

I f you've ever planned a birthday party, you can organize a mother-daughter book club.

I don't mean to make it sound overly easy. It does take some careful thought and planning. But organizing a book club is actually simpler than the administrative job most of us do each week to juggle everyone's schedules and expectations. And there are some very nice differences: First, the organizing task itself is something enjoyable to do with your daughter. And second, unlike the cluttered closets, family meals or after-school activity schedule, your book club needs to be organized only once!

In *The Important Book,* Margaret Wise Brown describes aspects of everyday life in their essential terms. "The important thing about the sky," she writes, "is that it is always there. It is true that it is blue, and high, and full of clouds, and made of air. But the important thing about the sky is that it is always there."

It helps to think about your Mother-Daughter Book Club in its essential terms right from the start. What is "the most important thing" about your club? What do you want it to do for you?

"The books are long and they're boring in the beginning. But they get interesting in the middle and the end."

BRITTNEY

My reasons for wanting to start a book discussion club were fairly straightforward. I saw a mother-daughter book club as a way to spend some special time with Morgan doing something that would get us talking and listening to each other and enjoying the company of other mothers and daughters with similar reading interests.

Think about your reasons. Whatever they are, it's important that you keep them in mind as you organize your club, inviting members, establishing meeting times, compiling a book list from which the girls will choose their selections. Each of these choices will influence the personality of your club and the direction it takes over time. Each step deserves some careful thought.

Tips from the Girls on Organizing a Mother~Daughter Book Club

"Let anyone join who wants to join, but don't get it too big, because the hostess has to cook all the food for refreshments."

— BRITTNEY

"Have good number of people because sometimes some people don't show up."

— JIHAN

"I would plan to have the girls close in age or grade. There is a big difference between a sixth grader and a fourth grader, in terms of their interests and reading abilities. However, it has been nice to get to know and socialize with the younger girls in our book club."

— REBECCA

Your Mother~Daughter Partnership: Ready, Set...

First impressions are important. The way you introduce the idea of the mother-daughter book club to your daughter may make or break your case, so think about the best way to present it to get the response you want—that excited "yes!"

We all bring more enthusiasm to things when we feel we've made a choice to be involved. The partnership you need with your daughter to start a mother-daughter book club will work only if your daughter wants to do it. If your daughter routinely rejoices at your suggestions for how she should spend her free time, then consider yourself indeed blessed and carry on. If, however, your daughter routinely or even occasionally resists activities you request, or even those you simply suggest, then don't do either. Try wondering out loud.

> *"Nobody ever says, 'That's dumb.' The moms and girls encourage each other."*
>
> JOYCE

In politics, they call it "floating a trial balloon." To test a potentially controversial idea at a safe distance from any negative fallout, politicians will see to it that somebody leaks the idea to the media. If it gets a positive response, they run up to claim it and carry it forward. If it gets a negative response, they listen from a distance and use the criticism to guide them as they modify the idea for a more successful introduction.

For mothers, that process boils down to one step: Choose words that make it easy for your daughter to say yes. If your experience is anything like mine, that means making an idea attractive to your daughter, never minding all the reasons that make it an attractive idea to you.

For example, here are two different ways to suggest to your daughter that you two start a mother-daughter book club. As you read them, imagine your daughter's reaction:

Mother: "I've got a great idea. Let's start a mother-daughter book club. We can assign books that are better literature than those paperbacks you read all the time. It'll give us all a chance to talk about the really important issues in life. And when you hear the other mothers' opinions, you'll see I'm not the only one who thinks the way I do."

I can hear the footsteps fade as she runs in the other direction.

Mother: "What would you think of inviting a group of your friends and their moms to read books, and then have a get-together with refreshments where you girls could relax and we'd all get to share what we thought about the story and do some fun activity with it?"

Style #2 was my choice, and Morgan took off running—to get the pencil and paper to make her list and start her invitations.

"I thought it was a good idea because usually you don't get to spend a lot of time with your mom, so I liked having something where I could spend time with my mom and with my friends," Morgan says.

What if your daughter hands you a negative response even with a positive introduction? She wouldn't be the first skeptic in the crowd.

"I thought, 'Oh no, here goes another thing,'" recalls Brittney. "I thought piano was going to be fun, and it turned out not to be. I thought basketball was going to be fun, and it turned out not to be. I thought soccer and softball were going to be fun, and they weren't. And I thought swimming was supposed to be fun, and it turned out to be quite boring. So I thought, 'Oh no, another thing I have to go to.'"

If your daughter balks, find out why. Listen to her reasons. You may discover that she doesn't understand the idea or thinks

BOOKS BRING MOTHER~DAUGHTER MEMORIES TO MIND...

My mother died when I was only five, but one of my memories of my mother was seeing her sitting down reading a book, and in order to get her attention I would run my hand up the page of the book she was reading, and watch her eyes. When my hand got her attention she would look up and see me.

After my mother died, we went to live with our grandmother in the South, and we didn't have a radio or access to a newspaper on a regular basis, but we would read everything we could get our hands on. My uncle was a schoolteacher, and we read his books. I still have a strong appreciation for geography because one of his books was a geography book and I remember reading it as much as I could. He'd bring fish wrapped up in newspaper and we would read the newspaper!

— BERTHA WATERS

Member, Federal Advisory Commission of the Mary McLeod Bethune Council House National Historic Site, a licensed social worker and professional consultant presenting parent-training and women's history programs

it would be more challenging or demanding than it really is. You may discover that she has personal reservations about reading or about socializing that deserve your attention. You both may discover that through talking about her response, you can identify the parts of the idea that *do* sound exciting, and use those to define the terms for your mother-daughter book club. If she really seems opposed to the idea, then drop it! Suggest the idea to another mother, and see if your daughter changes her mind when she gets an invitation in the mail to join her friends.

"Our Mother-Daughter Book Club has been everything I thought it might be, and maybe a little more, because I didn't imagine in the beginning that the girls would bring about the depth of discussion that they have."

ALICE

My point here is not to tell you how to talk with your daughter, but to suggest that our efforts to communicate with our daughters work best when we try to see the moment through their eyes. That's a big part of what the Mother-Daughter Book Club is about—listening to our girls and truly sharing the experience instead of directing it. As a woman and mother with a take-charge habit, it has taken me some time, and practice, to learn when to hit my pause button and listen: *listen* to my daughter's words and, with a caring heart, *hear* what she is saying.

Once the idea has the unanimous approval of the two of you, it's time to find some good company.

GIRL BY GIRL, MOM BY MOM: BUILDING A DISCUSSION GROUP

We're always instructing our girls to be inclusive, to keep the circle open as they play at recess or after school, or as they make their way through life. And I bristle when I hear about girls and cliques at school, or remember them from my own girlhood.

BOOKS TO GROW ON

I've simply selected books that I enjoyed reading at the time and that I find returning to my thoughts again and again. All of the books are thought-provoking and should be great discussion books. They range from serious to whimsical, from fact to fantasy. Although *Mrs. Mike*, published in 1947, may seem a bit out of place, I had to include it as it was my favorite book as a young girl. I first read it when I was in sixth grade and continued to read it at least once a year well into college.

Mrs. Mike, Benedict Freedman

The Giver, Lois Lowry

The Man from the Other Side, Uri Orlev

Dealing with Dragons, Patricia C. Wrede

Louisa May: The World and Works of Louisa May Alcott, Norma Johnston

Grace, Jill Paton Walsh

The Bomb, Theodore Taylor

Running Out of Time, Margaret Peterson Haddix

—BARBARA J. MCKILLIP, FOUNDER AND PRESIDENT,

The Libri Foundation

So when Morgan and I sat down to discuss who to invite to be in our Mother-Daughter Book Club, the fact that we were "picking" people seemed right and wrong at the same time. Why not invite all of Morgan's closest friends? Why not include those mothers with whom I had a close friendship, even if the girls weren't particularly close? Our "open door" policy had always served us well in the past. Why select a group now?

For the answer, go back to your original reasons for wanting to start a mother-daughter book club. For us, one of my motivations was the thought that this group would give Morgan and me an opportunity to spend time with each other and some friends we didn't see very often, exploring a common element of our lives—our African-American heritage. At first we planned to focus completely on books by African-American authors or about the black experience. Our reading selections quickly expanded beyond that original idea, to reflect our full range of interests. But the composition of the group—all African-American mothers and daughters—has become a wonderful source of support and experience of our cultural heritage, a theme that is missing from the girls' school programs and extracurricular activities, where they most often are a small racial minority.

Whatever your vision for the group, whether you plan to invite only girls and mothers you know well, or post your invitation on a library or Sunday school bulletin board for an open enrollment, you're hoping that the individuals who respond will be a "good fit." That doesn't mean they should all think alike. It

---

BOOKS TO
GROW ON

These are books from my childhood that I still love to read:

The Bible

Winnie the Pooh,
A. A. Milne

The Secret Garden,
Frances Hodgson Burnett

The Yearling,
Marjorie Kinnan Rawlings

A Tale of Two Cities,
Charles Dickens

—KATHERINE PATERSON, AUTHOR
Bridge to Terabithia

does mean that they need to share the vision or goals you have for your group, they should be able to participate in the group's reading, discussion and activities in a meaningful way and they should be able to follow through on any commitment they make to host or help coordinate the group meetings.

Some qualities that contribute to a "good fit" include:

* An interest in reading

* Reading skill level that makes reading a pleasurable activity

* Age or grade level close to the others

* Maturity level in the range necessary to participate fully in the reading, discussion and related activities

* Comfort in discussion

* A cooperative attitude

* An acquaintance or friendship with others in the group

* An interesting mix of viewpoints for the mothers, including differences of opinion shaped by each woman's life experience. It's best if every mother can be up front about any personal sensitivities—religious, political or otherwise—that would influence her enjoyment of the group or otherwise affect the group.

* If you want to create a group that shares a special interest or objective, think of girls who bring that particular life experience or reading interest to the group. (See Chapter Nine: "Using Themes to Guide Choices.")

This process of selecting who to invite is an opportunity to help your daughter learn about team building. They get plenty of experience in team*work* in their other school and after-school activities: cooperative learning projects at school, dance class, soccer teams, Girl Scouts. All of them offer wonderful opportunities for girls to gather together and experience the challenges and

Books to Grow On

Over the years there have been a number of books that my daughters and I have enjoyed. The following is a list of some of our favorites:

Little Women, Louisa May Alcott
Anne Frank: The Diary of a Young Girl, Anne Frank
Charlotte's Web, E. B. White
The Nancy Drew series, Carolyn Keene
Little House on the Prairie, Laura Ingalls Wilder

I also recommend the biographies of such influential women as Eleanor Roosevelt, Olympic legend Wilma Rudolph, and Susan B. Anthony, and also the writings of Maya Angelou. The lives of these women can serve as a source of inspiration to us all.

— TIPPER GORE
Office of the Vice President of the United States

delights of playing, performing or working toward a goal in a cooperative way.

Team *building* is different. It requires that you think about your goal and think about the qualities needed for the team to work well. In terms of a mother-daughter book club, it's important to aim for a lively yet harmonious blend of personalities and talents. All of our friends have special qualities. It's a matter of thinking about them, and tapping those girls and mothers who seem most likely to enjoy, and enable others to enjoy, good books, relaxed socializing and stimulating discussion.

This is another opportunity to listen to our daughters and show some trust, be willing to take a chance on their judgment. Morgan was absolutely determined that one of her younger friends—an eight-year-old girl who was not an avid reader—be invited to join the group. I resisted at first, believing that she simply wasn't quite ready to participate in a book discussion group. As it turned out, the mother and daughter were so enthusiastic about the idea that both were willing to put in extra effort to tackle the challenging reading assignments. And the perspectives and creativity they have brought to the group are cherished. Morgan *knew*; I listened and learned.

The More the Merrier...
Up to a Point

When you've got your list of names ready, it's time to do a little simple math. How many girls and mothers should you invite to establish your club?

I can share the advice of experts: The Great Books Foundation, in its suggestions for organizing book discussion groups for young people, suggests starting with eight to ten children. Teachers have recommended that from six to ten or so children makes a group small enough to be comfortable yet large enough to keep a discussion going strong.

I happen to be at ease with large groups, especially a group

A Special Place for Sharing and Growing Together

Reading together is a wonderful idea because it's a positive way to grapple with real-life issues. If these things come up in the context of a book, or a book discussion, then it doesn't seem so personal and it may be easier for the girls to discuss. It feels a little safer. And if the moms are open and they really want to hear what their girls are saying, then there can be a real sharing. You need to watch what the girls do, listen to them and understand that they are different than we are.

And the girls should be open and listening to what the mothers have to say, too. There is definitely something to learn from both sides.

An all-girl environment such as the one found in the Girl Scouts works so well because there girls really have a chance to be leaders, to show their leadership qualities, be creative, have a real voice and not be concerned about what a boy will say or have to defer to a boy because of the social pressure. With other girls, a girl feels comfortable trying out different roles and ways of expressing herself.

A girl needs to be able to say what she's really feeling—not just what she's "supposed to feel" or "the right thing"—but what she really feels, who she really is.

The most important thing mothers need to do is really express how much they care about their daughters. They need to show them that. They need to really listen to them and say, "Who is my daughter?"

rather than trying to make her into something. And, of course, enjoy—really enjoy her. Parents sometimes take an almost businesslike approach to living instead of looking for ways to have fun together.

It's also very important for girls growing up to have a sense that it's not just their mother who cares, but other adults who care and take them seriously. A Girl Scout leader or someone else's mother could do all those things.

— HARRIET S. MOSATCHE, PH.D., DEVELOPMENTAL PSYCHOLOGIST.
Director of Program Development, Girl Scouts of the U.S.A.

of girls and women I already know. Even so, when Morgan's list topped out at twenty girls, we managed to whittle it to a more realistic twelve invitations that went out in the next day's mail. One of the mothers in our group has told me since that when she first heard that invitations had gone out to that many girls, she had second thoughts about joining. Her daughter was one of the youngest in the group, a little shy and not an avid recreational reader. And the thought of eventually hosting a club meeting that brought twenty-four girls and moms into her home was daunting. Still, she and her daughter came for that first meeting and were pleasantly surprised to find that the number of mothers and daughters who actually signed on was quite comfortable.

While you're thinking about numbers, think again about the vision you have for your club. If having the club meet at members' homes is important to you, then you'll need to aim for a number that fits comfortably in your home settings.

For us, meeting at homes was important because it was where we felt we could most completely relax, reflect and enjoy our discussion. Over time, we also have come to realize that, for us, sharing our homes has been a way of sharing ourselves, and it gives the girls, especially, a tangible feeling of ownership of the club when they host a meeting. When one of our members felt her townhouse couldn't handle the crowd comfortably, she asked a friend for the use of *her* home. The request was graciously granted.

The ideal number will be small enough to fit comfortably in your meeting place and large enough to sustain a lively discussion even when a few are absent. I suggest inviting about four more girls than the minimum you would hope to have at every meeting. Then if someone misses, or one drops out, you still have a strong core group to keep your club going.

Sample Invitation

SHIREEN AND HER DAUGHTER
MORGAN
INVITE YOU TO
THE ORGANIZING MEETING OF
THE MOTHER-DAUGHTER BOOK CLUB

Sunday, October 1, 1995

Time: 4 to 6 P.M.

Place: Home of Alexis and
Jamexis Christian

RSVP: Shireen or Morgan Fykes

Please bring book ideas and your
calendar!

Taking the Lead: How Much Should You Plan in Advance?

When I organize something, I don't like to leave much to chance. So before we sent out our invitations, I called several mothers to be sure they were interested in doing this with us. We talked about the kinds of books we thought would be on-target for our group. And we agreed upon a convenient date for our organizational meeting.

From the moment I knew we were going to do this club, I began scouting the bookstores for books the group might want to read. I must have read fifteen or twenty books in my search for the eight that eventually were introduced to the girls. (See Chapter Four: "How to Find and Read Books.") But my efforts as a previewer paid off for the group. By the time we met for our organizational meeting, we had a good array of books from which the girls could pick one to start, and that made their selection process fairly simple.

There are other ways to blaze the trail to your first meeting and book selection. You might pick the first book yourself and include a copy of it—or simply name it—in the invitation that goes out to your charter members. Then, at your organizational meeting, the group can enjoy its first "official" mother-daughter book discussion.

Every book discussion group is bound to be unique, reflecting the age of its members, their interests and their life experiences. But our hunt for good books begins at the same place and leads us in the same direction. A wonderful thing—another pleasant surprise—comes out of the process of organizing, of looking for books, reading them and thinking about the girls, the mother-daughter relationship, the club, the stories and the discussions to come. It becomes absolutely clear that in the hubbub of all this living and literature, a mother-daughter book club is a *right* idea, one that brings us heart to heart, and the prospect of that first meeting becomes truly exciting.

BOOKS TO GROW ON

Ten of my favorite books when I was ten years old:

The Wizard of Oz, L. Frank Baum

Baby Island, Carol Ryrie Brink

Caddie Woodlawn, Carol Ryrie Brink

The Secret Garden, Frances Hodgson Burnett

Understood Betsy, Dorothy Canfield

James and the Giant Peach, Roald Dahl

The Peterkin Papers, Lucretia P. Hale

Misty of Chincoteague, Marguerite Henry

Mary Poppins, P. L. Travers

Stuart Little, E. B. White

Ten books I would now recommend to ten-year-olds:

Sounder, William H. Armstrong

The Secret Garden, Frances Hodgson Burnett

Ramona the Pest, Beverly Cleary

James and the Giant Peach, Roald Dahl

Anne Frank: The Diary of a Young Girl, Anne Frank

A Wrinkle in Time, Madeleine L'Engle

Rascal, Sterling North

Bridge to Terabithia, Katherine Paterson

Roll of Thunder, Hear My Cry, Mildred Taylor

Stuart Little, E. B. White

— ANN MARTIN, AUTHOR
The Baby-sitters Club series

ENDNOTES

★ Stay focused on your reasons for starting a mother-daughter book club.

★ Present the idea of a mother-daughter book club to your daughter as fun.

★ Choose members who share your vision and goals for the club.

CHAPTER THREE

THE ORGANIZATIONAL MEETING: PRELUDE TO A GREAT YEAR

For Ashley, the thought of a Sunday afternoon get-together with friends,

and of us reading the same book and actually spending time

reflecting together was just very exciting.

— GRACE SPEIGHTS

ASHLEY & GRACE SPEIGHTS

Hi, my name is Ashley Speights, I'm ten years old and am in fifth grade at National Cathedral School. I have three pets. They are my dog Snowball, my guinea pig Heineken and my cat Nosey. I also have a brother, Nathaniel, who is seven. My hobbies are collecting seashells and stickers. I like music, and I play the piano and the guitar. I also like to play sports like basketball, tennis and volleyball. I'm a Girl Scout. In my spare time I like to visit with friends, play with my dog and read.

I used to be pretty shy, but when I started school at NCS—it's all girls—I began to feel more comfortable talking in front of people. Now my mother says I never stop talking!

My favorite authors are Roald Dahl, Lois Lowry and R. L. Stine. My favorite book by Roald Dahl is *George's Marvelous Medicine*. My favorite book by Lois Lowry is *Anastasia Has the Answers*, and my brother and I have all of Stine's Goosebumps books. One of my other favorite books is *Island of the Blue Dolphins* by Scott O'Dell.

My mother's name is Grace and she is thirty-nine. She and my dad are both lawyers. My mom travels a lot, but she also comes to my things at school and reads with me. We're lucky because my grandmother—my mom's mother—lives with us.

Mom and I like the Mother-Daughter Book Club so much because we get to do things we both like a lot—reading, being together and talking with our friends. I enjoy snuggling up with my mom to read our book club books together. It is a very special time for me.

I can still feel Morgan's bubbly excitement and remember my own cheerful expectations the night of our organizational meeting. I felt akin to Noah—or perhaps to Mrs. Noah—as two by two they arrived, mothers and daughters. With each tap at the front door, two more beaming smiles, two more partners welcomed into the slowly growing group in the family room. The sound of girls' and women's warm laughter and conversation wafted through the house like holiday music. It felt good. This is the way it should be, I thought: A happy conspiracy of girls and women, books, conversation and sharing.

No matter how familiar everyone is with everyone, we all enjoy a simple icebreaker activity that welcomes us to a new, special circle. The one I chose for our organizational meeting was deceptively simple: Each girl was asked to introduce her mother and tell a little about her, and each mother was asked to do the same for her daughter. Well! Those simple introductions launched us into some remarkable discussion and discovery.

Morgan, for instance, told the group that I worked at the Smithsonian Institution, which is true, but her sense of what I did there was thin on detail: "She mostly sits in a little office and answers the telephone," Morgan volunteered, "and then she comes home and changes clothes and goes out to parties a lot." In my work as a museum administrator, coordinating exhibits and events for the Smithsonian Institution's Center for African American History and Culture, I suppose I *do* sit in my office and talk on the telephone quite a bit. And I *am* expected to represent the Smithsonian—and other organizations

> ### BOOKS TO GROW ON
>
> *The Twenty-One Balloons,*
> William P. Du Bois
>
> *Anne of Green Gables,*
> Lucy M. Montgomery
>
> *Ozma of Oz,*
> L. Frank Baum
>
> *Homer Price,*
> Robert McCloskey
>
> *Centerburg Tales,*
> Robert McCloskey
>
> *Anne Frank:*
> *The Diary of a Young Girl,*
> Anne Frank
>
> —NORA EPHRON, NOVELIST,
> SCREENWRITER, DIRECTOR
> *Heartburn, When Harry Met Sally*

MOTHERS & DAUGHTERS:
APPRECIATING THE DIFFERENCES

We all want to be appreciated for who we are. Daughters want
some positive mirroring from their parents—to be seen and heard for
who they are and what they are. Mirroring is shorthand meaning somebody really sees the other person—taking in what the other person is
putting out, and communicating that we're taking it in. It's like saying, "I
hear you," rather than "Why can't you do it the way I did?"

Almost everyone thinks of their life as a rough draft and their
child's life as an edited version—and they will be the editor. Of course,
people don't articulate it that way. But it's a shock when you discover
you're not working from the same manuscript. In these times we live in,
when the pace of change is so rapid, the kid's manuscript changes very
rapidly.

The pace of life itself is not as leisurely as it used to be. Any one
member of a family is connected to an electronic device at any given
moment—TV, computer, video game—there really isn't unstructured
time for easy talk, random talk, for wide-ranging conversations about this
or that.

But with a mother-daughter book club, here's this golden opportunity for girls to hear. It's almost like a literary version of the quilting
bees, where the little ones would listen and women would talk, which is
a terrific way of transmitting wisdom. But the reality is that our children
are growing up in the age of the sound bite and MTV, and that's why it's
so important that the group is daughter-focused—why it needs to be

daughter-focused or they'll lose interest.

Instead of lecturing or pushing your point, it can be useful to point out that you're surprised by the girls' reaction to something: "We thought you would have a lot to say about this or that, but you seemed to move right over it." The girls can ask themselves why, and the girls can tell the moms why they didn't think it was so interesting. That's an opportunity for real contact.

—SUMRU ERKUT, PH.D.
Associate Director of the Center for Research on Women, Wellesley College

on whose boards I serve—at many cultural events, often in the evening. But the reality of my work is quite different from the impression that Morgan had developed from her vantage point.

The other mothers enjoyed similar revelations as we discovered, introduction by introduction, that what we did with the days of our lives was not necessarily clear to our daughters. With every introduction—mothers and daughters alike—came some opportunity to set a record straight ("Mom, I don't enjoy music, I take music lessons—it's not the same thing!")

We had great fun with it, but I can tell you as well that it was a perfect lesson in sharing and discovery between the mothers and daughters there. All without a single lecture!

This is also a perfect time to poll each girl on the types of books she enjoys the most. The answers can help guide your search for new titles to bring to her. And her involvement in that process adds to her sense of ownership in the club and the book selection process.

Because the mothers in our Mother-Daughter Book Club had so much in common it was easy to agree upon some basic objectives of our group. Thus, the business—I like to call it *housekeeping*—part of our organizational meeting was fairly

---

BOOKS TO GROW ON

The Nancy Drew series,
Carolyn Keene (my childhood favorites)

The Giving Tree
Shel Silverstein

What's Happening to Me?
Where Did I Come From?
Peter Mayle

Value Tale series
Ann D. Johnson and
Spencer Johnson

The Prophet
Khalil Gibran

Roll of Thunder, Hear My Cry
Mildred D. Taylor

Their Eyes Were Watching God
Zora Neale Hurston

Go Ask Alice
Anonymous

Catcher in the Rye
J. D. Salinger

Are You There God? It's Me Margaret
Judy Blume

Stuart Little
E. B. White

The Ramona series
Beverly Cleary

—FAYE WATTLETON
The Center for Gender Equality

short. I welcomed the group, described my reasons for wanting to establish the club, and asked the members whether they were ready to commit to it for themselves. The answer was a resounding yes, and we were on our way.

Since there are several points that need to be covered in that initial setting-up discussion, it helps to have a mental agenda, or some notes to keep the group on track, making progress. But there's no need to have a formal agenda to hand out, there's no need to have elected officers and there's no need to run the meetings like a business seminar.

"I thought this sounded like a great idea—it sounded like fun to get to know my mom."

MORGAN

Remember, the important thing about a mother-daughter book club is the sharing and discussion. You don't really *need* a lot of structure, rules and regulations. Any structure to the group should be for the sole purpose of simplifying the effort so you can focus on enjoying books and one another. Don't worry about building in opportunities for leadership, responsibility and cooperative effort. In a mother-daughter book club, it *all* happens— *naturally*.

That said, for some minimal structure, points for the group to review and agree upon might include:

✷ **The general purpose and philosophy of the club.**

✷ **Responsibilities beyond reading,** such as hosting or researching authors if that's something you want done regularly.

✷ **A leader or coordinator** to facilitate the housekeeping part of the meetings. I've served in that role for our group since I organized it, but it may make sense to rotate that duty, perhaps yearly, among any mothers willing to handle it.

✷ **Whether you want to lead the discussion yourselves** or consider asking a professional facilitator to do it. Our girls do it themselves. But expert facilitators, often available through the

THE CALENDAR CRUNCH—
WHEN TO MEET

There isn't a day in the week when most of us have long stretches of time unclaimed and available for a relaxing get-together.

A few tips may help you carve out the calendar space you need to enjoy a mother-daughter book club.

✳ **Establish the length of the meeting and stick with it.** Start and end on time as a matter of courtesy to the hosting mothers, as well as others who have families or other commitments waiting at home. It's easier to imagine making the time for the meeting if you can depend on it to ask no more of you.

"You want to be careful to keep it simple and not let the food or activities get so complicated that your meetings run over the time you've set aside. When it runs longer, you're running into family time," says Cheryl.

✳ **Allow ample time for home reading between meetings.** Once a month provides a nice stretch of time for reading amid all the other commitments we have. You may need to schedule meetings a little closer or farther apart at times to accommodate holidays and other calendar conflicts. Or you may want to make the meetings quarterly simply because that's the schedule that's most comfortable for you.

✳ **If you meet after school, see if carpooling can simplify the pick-up process at school,** while off-duty moms drive straight to the meeting house. This makes getting there a little less hectic for the off-duty moms, and a rotating car pool duty means the driving isn't a big deal for anyone most of the time. If your girls go to different schools, look for meeting times that take everyone's situation into consideration.

✶ **If weekends are a "family time" for you,** look for a pocket of in-between time when your absence for a couple of hours won't be missed so much. For instance, our group began meeting the first Sunday of every month, from 2 to 4 p.m. We've expanded it to 3 to 6 p.m. to allow for more social time, but that's remained a comfortable commitment for most of us most of the time.

✶ **Expect that everyone will miss a meeting from time to time.** It's virtually impossible to accommodate everyone's schedule all of the time. If you plan to be absent, however, let the hosting mother and daughter know as soon as possible so they can plan accordingly.

public library or a bookstore, can be a good idea, especially for a larger, community-based mother-daughter book club.

* **Meeting dates.** The simplest way is to pick a schedule as a group and stick with it. We established the first Sunday afternoon of each month as our set meeting date. We scheduled around a couple of major conflicts—a Girl Scout camp out and a national holiday—but otherwise we stick to the plan. That little bit of structure establishes the meeting—and the group—as a priority for one day each month. It means we aren't constantly checking with each other to confirm when the next meeting is, or trying to negotiate changes to accommodate all the variables in everyone's lives. Inevitably, someone can't make it to a meeting now and then. That's life.

* **A book selection process.** (See Chapter Four: "How to Find and Read Books.")

* **Hosting duty.** Members can sign up for the date that suits them for hosting the Mother-Daughter Book Club, whether it's at their home or an alternative location. Sometimes someone picks a date because they have a special interest in the book—perhaps they recommended it—or a book-related activity. Hosting duty means providing refreshments, being prepared to lead the discussion, and, if you wish, planning a book-related activity. (See Chapter Ten: "Beyond the Books.")

* **Expectations,** such as that mothers and daughters attend together, and that both read the book and be prepared to share thoughts about it.

Whatever you do, remember your objectives for the club and the personality of your group. Let your structure and your choices reflect the true desires of the group. Be candid about preferences. Even the discussions of planning details can lead to interesting insights into each other's lives if only we are honest about our feelings.

For instance, if you want the girls to explore new titles—

ones that none of the girls has yet read—then the mothers may want to facilitate by providing book options, allowing the girls to make the final choice. There's no need to lecture the girls about the need for mothers to pick out "what's good for them." By contributing to the selection process, you're showing them that you can help them access the world and they can make good choices. It can be a win-win situation.

Depending on the age and interests of the girls, it may work out fine for them to have a more specific say in finding and selecting the titles for the group. Or you may want to ask each mother-daughter team to be responsible for selecting a book and hosting the meeting for that discussion. That gives each girl the chance to see her special choice become the group's pick, but allows for some motherly input in the process. However you decide to pick the club's books, be prepared to experiment with it a bit and let it evolve to reflect the desires of your group.

A nice touch for the organizational meeting is to have take-home materials prepared for each mother-daughter couple. This might be an article of interest from the newspaper, a list of the year's Caldecott Medal, Coretta Scott King, or Newbery awards for children's literature, or simply:

✴ **The club membership list,** with names, addresses and phone numbers

✴ **A list of phone numbers** of area bookstores, libraries or other helpful community contacts

✴ **The initial suggested book list** for the group

✴ **Any reminders**

If supplying these materials is too costly or inconvenient, you might consider some simple alternatives:

✴ **Keep a Mother-Daughter Book Club scrapbook** for articles or information members bring to share. The materials can be read casually during the nondiscussion portion of the meeting.

SURPRISES—EVEN AMONG FRIENDS: BREAKING THE ICE

The warmest of friends can still enjoy an icebreaker activity to get a meeting off to a rousing start. Here are two winners:

Mother-Daughter Introductions:

Invite each mother to introduce her daughter, and each daughter to introduce her mom.

Suggest that everyone include a brief description of what the other does during the day, and then focus on qualities that make her daughter or mother special—no need to talk about "flaws" or shortcomings here!

Expect a round of giggles and groans from the girls, but don't let them squirm out of it. They'll love hearing nice things about themselves and saying nice things about their moms.

Once the introductions are made, go around the circle of girls and ask what kinds of books they like to read the most. The information will be useful later when the group wants to select new books to read.

To Tell the Truth (or Fiction and Nonfiction!):

Give each mother and daughter a piece of paper and pencil.

Ask everyone to write on the sheet four "facts" about themselves that the others, even close friends may not know—three of the comments should be true, but one should be false. The more believable the false statement is, the more fun the group has trying to sort out the possible truth from the possible fiction.

Going around the group one person at a time, ask each person to read all four of her "facts" aloud and let the group guess which one is false. To conclude her turn, each girl or woman reads her four statements again, this time disclosing whether the statement is true—nonfiction—or fiction.

You may choose to ask mother and daughters to play as partners, coming up with four statements that describe either or both of them— but one statement that is completely false for both.

This activity can be enjoyed more than once. Consider playing it again to add a sparkle to a midyear meeting.

✳ Make a do-it-yourself member list, by arranging the girls in a circle or a line, then giving each girl a sheet of paper and asking her to write her and her mother's name, address and phone number on a line or two. Ask the girls to pass their page on to the girl on their right and write the same information again on the page they now hold. Keep going until the pages have come full circle and each one contains the information from all the girls. Each girl will have a list with her name at the top!

YOU'RE A CLUB NOW: SEE YOU NEXT TIME!

In the sweet children's story *Corduroy*, a little stuffed bear bumbles from one place to another, optimistic but never quite certain if what he has found is the something that he had always imagined and wished for. Finally, at the end of one adventurous day, he guesses right: snuggled in the arms of a little girl who treasures him, Corduroy muses: "You must be a friend. I've always wanted to have a friend."

> *"It's kind of nice to have it at your house. You get to visit other people's houses, and it's nice to have them to yours."*
>
> JIHAN

By the end of our organizational meeting, Morgan and I felt as if we had truly found the thing that we previously had only imagined could exist. Before that meeting, our idea for a mother-daughter book club was just that: an idea. Now it was real! We had gathered together. We had talked. We had planned. We had enjoyed the meeting immensely. The enthusiasm within the circle of mothers and daughters was unanimous.

This must be a mother-daughter book club. And it was even better than we'd imagined!

Books to Grow On

CLASSICS:

Alice in Wonderland and *Through the Looking Glass,* Lewis Carroll

Jane Eyre, Charlotte Brontë

Selected Poems of Emily Dickinson

Little Women, Louisa May Alcott

Pride and Prejudice, Jane Austen

CONTEMPORARIES:

A Mother and Two Daughters, Gail Godwin

A Thousand Acres, Jane Smiley

Dinner at the Homesick Restaurant, Anne Tyler

Annie John, Jamaica Kincaid

Foxfire, Joyce Carol Oates

Mother's Love, Mary Morris

Needle's Eye, Margaret Drabble

Quilting: Poems 1987–1990, Lucille Clifton

The Mother Child Papers, Alicia Ostriker

—JOYCE CAROL OATES, NOVELIST, POET, CRITIC
We Were the Mulvaneys

A SAMPLE ORGANIZATIONAL PLAN
AND MEETING CHECKLIST

✶ **Think about objectives** to determine a group identity or theme-based interest.

✶ **Contact school or community librarians,** bookstore contacts and others for recommended reading. Contact a bookstore about discounts on group purchases.

✶ **Call ahead to a core group** of mothers and daughters to confirm sufficient interest. Send out invitations to those and others for an organizational meeting.

✶ **Arrange a potluck dinner or refreshments** for an organizational meeting.

✶ **Greetings**—describe the idea for the club and the vision, theme or philosophy you have in mind. Ask for show of hands or voice to signify approval or need for discussion.

✶ **Icebreaker Game:** Mother-Daughter Introductions or Fiction/Nonfiction games.

✶ **Establish your book selection process.** Choose the book for the next meeting, or pick the next two or three books as well, to eliminate the need to spend time on that process at every meeting.

✶ **Poll girls for interests** to guide future selections.

✷ **Set meeting dates and hours.**

✷ **Review host mother-daughter duties,** which are to provide meeting space and refreshments, prepare questions about the book to lead discussion and coordinate or supply materials for any book-related activity.

✷ **Create and distribute a member list** with telephone numbers and addresses.

✷ **Establish a club leader or coordinator** to monitor calendar changes and manage other minor coordinating duties for a year.

✷ **Ask for a volunteer mother and daughter** to serve as communicator, typing up highlights from each meeting to send out to absent members or calling them to let them know information needed for the following meeting.

ENDNOTES

✶ An icebreaking activity is a fun way to begin.

✶ Club meetings need minimal structure—sharing and discussion occur naturally.

✶ The basic organization of the club can reflect your group's personality and objectives.

✶ Include your daughter in the preparations for this and every other club meeting. It's a great way to spend time together.

CHAPTER FOUR

HOW TO FIND
AND READ BOOKS

Reading books really should be fun, you know.

It can't always be about improving, about learning lessons in life.

—PAM SACKS, *The Cheshire Cat Bookstore*

BRITTNEY & LESLYE FRASER

Hello, my name is Brittney Nicole Fraser. I'm ten years old and I live in Maryland. We moved here from California when I was in first grade. There are four people in my family: Mom, Dad, my brother Michael, who is seven, and myself. I'm the oldest child, like my mom.

My favorite hobbies are reading, swimming and playing on the computer. I also like to play chess and the piano. My least favorite activity is playing the flute. I'm in fifth grade this year at a math and science "magnet" school. I am very good at math, even if I don't actually like it so much.

In my life, I have been to six different schools. I've made good friends everywhere I've gone, so it's been kind of hard leaving them behind. I miss them. I got to know Holly, Morgan and Maya at our church, so the Mother-Daughter Book Club seemed like a good way to get to play with them some more and meet some new friends. It's a good idea to have more than one or two friends because sometimes a friend can be too busy to play, or sometimes you just don't feel like playing with someone because they haven't been acting friendly.

My mother's name is Leslye Miller Fraser. She is an attorney in the Office of General Counsel at the U.S. Environmental Protection Agency. Before she was a lawyer she was a chemical engineer, but then she decided she wanted to do something different, so she went to law school when I was two years old. Now she works on things that have to do with law and engineering, and I like the idea that she's helping people take care of the environment. My mom says that when she was little, she was a tomboy and a bookworm, like me. We both like to read a lot and sometimes we can't hear people talking to us when we're reading a good book. I read all the time—like when I'm supposed to be cleaning my room or sleeping.

My favorite books are the Baby-sitters series and Nancy Drew. My mom's favorite book is *Kane and Abel,* by Jeffrey Archer.

When I say that I scouted for books in that period before our group met for the first time, that's a dignified way of saying the thrill of the hunt took over my life. On my way to the office I'd stop at this bookstore or that one. I recruited help: my husband would return from his trips to the library laden with offerings from the helpful librarian. On business trips to different cities, I'd find the local bookstores specializing in children's or African American titles; I'd scour the book racks at airports and hotel gift shops. If a friend at the office or in the neighborhood recommended a book, I'd be off and running—and *reading*.

I'd like to be able to tell you that I found the perfect books for your mother-daughter book club or that by using the book lists I've collected here, you're all set. Instead, I'll share the two most important things I learned from my crash course in literature:

> *THING ONE:*
>
> *You really can't judge a book by looking at its cover—or even its reputation.*

> *THING TWO:*
>
> *Always be sure that one of the mothers in the group—or a trusted librarian, bookstore contact or other knowledgeable adviser—has read a book before you suggest it to your group.*

I discovered during my preliminary reading, for instance, that one book that *looked* ordinary enough and sounded interesting from the back cover description actually dealt with incest. There wasn't a clue on the cover of that book that the story included such a sensitive topic. Some classics were heavy with ignorant or stereotyped images of women or men, or of people of different races, religions or beliefs. Other books took a more enlightened view but treated complex issues in overly simplistic ways, with plots and characters that were just too tidy.

It's not that these books wouldn't provide points for discussion—of course, they would—but with our limited time together, we wanted to focus on literature that fueled the girls' excitement about reading, gave them some positive images of girls and women making their way in the world and affirmed their courage to be themselves.

"IT'S A GREAT BOOK"—SAYS WHO?

I love a good bookstore. Any place where books line the walls and fill every flat surface is a place where my heart is at home. Thousands of books all around and every one of them is a treasure, a real find, if you believe what you read on the promotional posters and book cover comments. In the presence of so many, how do you close in on the few, the books that hold particular promise of reading enjoyment and discussion for your mother-daughter book club?

I found Pam. Pam Sacks was our resourceful contact at the Cheshire Cat Bookstore, a gem of a neighborhood bookstore where I had shopped for children's books for years. She enjoyed being a matchmaker, suggesting books that would be a fit for this child or that one. When I told her about our Mother-Daughter Book Club, and our particular interests, she made a number of suggestions—about books, about children and about subject matter—so insightful that her wisdom guides us still today.

For instance, I told Pam that one of our goals was to strengthen our mother-daughter relationships, and that we'd like a book that would inspire some discussion along those lines. I was expecting her to recommend a book with a strong mother-daughter story to tell. She didn't. Instead, Pam suggested we read

> *"I like to think of what happens to characters in good novels and stories as knots—things keep knotting up.*
> *And by the end of the story—readers see an 'unknotting' of sorts. Not what they expect, not the easy answers you get on TV, not wash-and-wear philosophies, but a reproduction of believable emotional experiences."*
>
> TERRY MCMILLAN
> *Introduction,* Breaking Ice

The Man in the Ceiling by Jules Feiffer, a cartoonist, author and writer of plays and screenplays—and a man. The good-humored story includes a mother and two daughters, but the main character is Jimmy, a boy cartoonist who grapples with the creative struggle that is part of art and life. The story depicts family life from a child's frank perspective, complete with caring but self-absorbed parents and intentionally annoying, self-centered siblings.

Pam's explanation: The book was wonderfully written, and by focusing more on the little boy's experience of his entire family, especially an unsympathetic father, it would give us a way to *begin* to discuss parent-child relationships without confronting the mother-daughter relationship head-on. The presence of an interesting mother character in the book also carried some potential for discussion if the girls picked up on it.

And that's exactly what happened. All of us enjoyed the book thoroughly. The girls instantly picked up on issues dealing with the rivalry between brothers and sisters, and on how the family members communicated with each other. There was a lot of talk about family relationships and this child's emotional struggle to be himself in a family and world that were too busy to take him seriously. Then a few of the girls took the mother character to task for being "selfish" because she had this little room where she would go and work on her artwork, and she wasn't totally accessible to her kids when she was working there. And suddenly we were in the middle of a spirited discussion about mothers, and how it is that if the dad is a workaholic that's okay with everybody, but if the mom focuses on a work project then *she's* selfish. All of us had a good time with that one, and I know it's because the subject came up indirectly. *It was a book and it was somebody else's family.*

> *"Many women tell stories about what saved them from the precipice. One girl was saved by her love of books, by long summer afternoons when she read for hours."*
>
> DR. MARY PIPHER, AUTHOR
> *Reviving Ophelia*

BIOGRAPHIES:
SHARING THE CAN-DO SPIRIT

Every "famous woman" started out as the girl next door. Joan Franklin Smutny, educator, author and activist for child-centered education, suggests that the biographies of famous women, as well as the stories of other men and women who have accomplished remarkable things, carry a special message for our daughters.

Girls need to read stories of women who have done great things and women who have overcome tremendous obstacles—whether it's family background, poverty, educational circumstances, other limitations or external conditions. They need to see that others have done it.

Girls today need to hear mothers talk about their lives in everyday conversation. How they overcame adversity. How they managed to reach where they are—wherever they are.

We can help girls develop a sense of that higher vision, that feeling that says, "Of course I can," instead of accepting limitations on their talents or fields of interest. Too often girls themselves accept stereotypes about the college or career choices in which they can expect to be successful. They need to see beyond the traditional opportunities and see that women have achieved greatness in math, science, computers, engineering, law or medicine.

Girls are desperately seeking values. Biographies emit them. When you read the life of a great person, or a person who has struggled, for discussion, you can ask:

* Why is this person a great person?

* What did this person contribute to his or her community and the world?

* What were the adversities they met along the way, and how did they overcome those adversities?

* When they were young, did everyone like them? Were they considered successful and popular?

* How did those experiences prepare them to make the contribution they did?

* What were their qualities: their strengths and weaknesses. How did they overcome their weaknesses?

I think that biography encapsulates values as almost nothing else can. Every family has its own values, but in a larger sense, we all want children to aspire. We want our children to say, "It can be done, I can do it." A biography says just exactly that: "I did it, and this is what I had to do to do it." And the good biography tells a child, "You can do it, too."

Pam's familiarity with children's literature and the way children interact with literature proved an invaluable guide. It helped us understand that sometimes the best approach to an issue is *indirect*, through literature that offers a nonthreatening arena—one with some distance built in—for discussing ideas that otherwise hit very close to home.

Because our Mother-Daughter Book Club members had a special desire to explore more African American literature, Pam also identified authors and books she felt would be of particular interest to us. That's how we discovered Virginia Hamilton, much-acclaimed author of stories that give young readers the intellectual respect they are due.

Whether you look to a favorite bookstore contact, a community librarian or other adviser for suggestions, your most valuable advice will come from people who know and understand what you're looking for—as well as what you're *not* looking for.

We've found that it works well when one of the mothers in our group can "preread" a book and share the story and her impressions of it with us during our moms' portion of the meeting, before we add it to the group of books from which the girls will choose. The previewing activity is fun, and it gives us another way to share a facet of our thinking. Ultimately, it means that even when we drop a book because it isn't a good fit, we've gained insights just from discussing the book and issues it raises.

BOOKS TO GROW ON

Favorite books in my youth:

The Wind in the Willows,
Kenneth Grahame

The Wizard of Oz,
L. Frank Baum

Smoky, the Cow Horse,
Will James

Little Women,
Louisa May Alcott

Gone with the Wind,
Margaret Mitchell

—BETH WINSHIP,
SYNDICATED COLUMNIST
"Ask Beth"

MOTHERS:
SHARING, TRUSTING, READING

One of the delights of a book discussion group is that everyone brings a different point of view or a different life experience to share, and it's the mix that keeps the talk simmering along. That same intellectual energy can spark some friction when it comes to selecting books, particularly among the mothers. No matter how much you may have in common—friendship, work, religion, ethnic heritage—you're bound to find some differences regarding basic issues you just may never have chatted about before. These kinds of differences can arise over any aspect of a book—the author, the writing style or language, the plot, the theme, the characters, imagery and race or gender issues.

Language was an interesting point of discussion in our early reviews of selections to put before the girls. Initially, several mothers wanted to avoid books in which the African-American characters spoke regional dialects or slang, rather than conventional American English. Others felt the dialects were valuable *if* they contributed to the authenticity of the characters and to the reader's overall experience of the story. After some discussion we all agreed that the quality of the literature should be our guide.

> *"I just wrote the kind of books I wanted to read as a child."*
>
> BEVERLY CLEARY
> *Ramona books*

Through our discussion, the mothers in the group were able to share feelings and explore issues in a way we don't often get the chance to do waiting in car pool lines or on the sidelines of a soccer field. The discussion was interesting in itself, and it helped each of us understand the other just a little better.

Sometimes, as mothers, our feelings vary about different subject matter. It may be that we aren't comfortable with the subject, or it may be that we don't feel it's appropriate reading—just yet, anyway—for *our* daughter. Or it may be a matter of timing: when one father in our group was seriously ill, we decided against one particular book because the death of the father character was

ON CHOOSING WOMEN AUTHORS

I once had a furious argument with a college president over a book list—I said it needed more women authors. He said, "We do *Anna Karenina*, by Leo Tolstoy and all these other books that have women characters." But all the writers were male. "There is a difference," I said, and he started to scream!

The fact that Louisa May Alcott or Jane Austen or other women writers' names are on a book is a very important statement, and we should talk about that: how things were for women writers. Girls need to know what it was like, historically, for women to write. Why, in the Renaissance if a daughter wrote a poem and it was published, it was as shameful as if she had run naked down the street. Women weren't supposed to write. The Renaissance was no renaissance for women.

People will point to books written *about* women, by men, and books written *by* women, and say, "Tell me, what is the difference?" The answer, in addition to the fact that women will be portrayed differently, is to say, "Well, how many books do you know where female friendships are *authentically* portrayed, where childbirth is *really* portrayed, where the mother-daughter relationship is talked about in a *meaningful* way, where women's *real* experience during wartime is portrayed? You could look at what's left out." Virginia Woolf said it so well in *A Room of One's Own*: "Women are inevitably portrayed in men's literature as having to do with men; their lives are seen as centered on men. And how little of a woman's life this is!"

Women have very full lives, and while love and romance may be part of it, they are hardly the center of it everyplace but in the movies. It's very important that girls get a sense of this, and they do get it in literature by women.

— ELLEN SILBER, PH.D.
Director of the Marymount Institute for the Education of Women and Girls

central to the book. We didn't avoid every book that included the death of a character. We simply were sensitive to any particular emotional pain or discomfort a story might impose on any one of us.

Beyond those special circumstances, we try not to shy away from great books with difficult or sensitive subjects, as long as the presentation is age-appropriate for our girls. (See Chapter Eight: "Girls Will Be Girls: Age and Attitudes.") When the group reads a good book that contains an element that we all anticipate will be a bit touchy, usually one of two things happens. Either the girls pick up on the topic and enjoy a spirited discussion of their views, or they skip right past that detail of the story to the aspects of the story that they find compelling to talk about.

> *"I was not a good reader as a young girl. I became a much better reader when I began reading to my children."*
>
> SUMRU ERKUT

Regardless of the nature of the discussion during group time, when we bring a book into our circle, we bring its story into our lives. We add its issues, its images, its messages to our thoughts. And the reflections can shimmer in conversation far removed from the circle. It may be during after-school or bedtime chat, or standing in line at the grocery store, but the ideas do surface again when their time is right.

CREATIVE CHOICES: NOVELS AREN'T THE ONLY BOOKS

Our continuing prowl for good books provides constant reminders that thought-provoking images and ideas come in all shapes and sizes. In our first year we focused on novels. That idea of a "book" seemed familiar and comfortable to the girls and mothers. Novels just seemed to provide the best story structure for discussion. Now that we're old hands at the art of discussion (and you'll be delighted at how quickly that transformation occurs!), we're getting more creative in how we look at—and look for—a good read.

What a field day! Biographies, poetry, short stories, essays, nonfiction and photo essays. Even picture books can open the doors of discussion in wonderful ways. The more we explore, the more we discover, about the world as well as about ourselves and each other.

READING LISTS: GREAT FOR BRAINSTORMING IDEAS

Books are a refreshing undercurrent of life and conversation almost anywhere I go. In my office, when we're gathered around the conference room table stuffing envelopes for the next event mailing, we're as likely to mention the book we're currently reading, or just finished, or read last year, or heard about from our mother-in-law, as we are any other topic of the day.

A few weeks later, there is always the follow-up conversation: "Did you get a chance to read that book yet? What did you think?" Regardless of the opinion, the discussion instantly taps into our feelings about characters, plots and ideas the book brought our way. Recommendations are always made with good intentions. Whether the book itself was a hit or a flop, the discussion is always refreshing.

The stream of books and recommendations for reading flows from ancient days, literally, with classics, proclaimed classics-to-be and books that promise a simple good read. Books may rise to fame, sink and surface again in the course of time and the changing context of culture and

> ### BOOKS TO GROW ON
>
> *The Souls of Black Folk*
> W. E. B. Du Bois
>
> *Narrative of the
> Life of Frederick Douglass*
> Frederick Douglass
>
> *Incidents in the Life of a Slave Girl*
> Harriet B. Jacobs
>
> *Colored People*
> Henry Louis Gates Jr.
>
> *Coming of Age in Mississippi*
> Anne Moody
>
> —HENRY LOUIS GATES JR.
> Professor of Humanities, Harvard
> University; editor, *The Norton Anthology of
> African American Literature*

On Life, Literature and the Pursuit of a Good Read

Reading at night, summer vacation—it was such an event to go to our library and check out the biggest stack of books I could carry. I'd read Nancy Drew, the Bobbsey Twins, horse stories by Marguerite Henry, light fantasy such as Doctor Dolittle books, *Mr. Popper's Penguins* and the Roald Dahl books. I loved my mother's Laura Ingalls Wilder books and E. B. White's books. I still have all my childhood books. When I was first leaving home the majority of cartons I packed were full of my books.

I was a pretty eclectic reader then and now, everything from the series books to the classics and in between. I love Stephen King and gobble his books up, and still read the classics, new fiction and nonfiction and short stories. I think that's how a lot of children read. If the Baby-sitters Club series is all a child is reading right now, I wouldn't be too concerned. I'm sure she's going to go on to something else. I do make sure to include in the Baby-sitters books other existing titles—if I need to mention a book because one of the characters has a book report or project due, I'll recommend one of my favorites for kids.

—ANN MARTIN, AUTHOR
The Baby-sitters Club series

readers' interests and expectations. With all the possibilities, it's always nice to hear suggestions from friends or others whose opinions we enjoy or respect. As you consider selections for your mother-daughter book club, tap into that reservoir of recommendations for ideas.

Reading lists are a wonderful way to find ideas for book selections and to share with others a title you feel is special. Our Cheshire Cat Bookstore friend Pam Sacks reminds us, however, that book lists should be used as a starting point rather than an assignment sheet.

"You can never foretell, you can never predict what the outcome is going to be of a reading experience."

NINA BAYM

"Reading lists should come with a Surgeon General's warning," Pam says. "Just because they were right for someone else doesn't make them right for you."

Pam also points out that reading lists can become dated in ways that affect their usefulness. Some titles go out of print and copies are difficult to find. Others may be easy to find but not really a match for your group's interests. Remember that "good books" are good for different reasons to different people. Pick and choose the selections based on your own group's interests.

FINDING BOOKS
THAT BELIEVE IN GIRLS

Not all "great" books are created equal. Some portray girls and women in ways that ignore the realities of our lives and those of women historically. There are reasons for it, of course.

Some books reflect an era when belittling comments or attitudes about women were the norm in the dominant culture. Other books, in casting boys and men as the action characters, simply leave women out of the picture or portray them as minor characters, when, in historical fact, they played active, important roles in the "story" of real life.

In her book *Woman's Fiction: A Guide to Novels by and about Women in America, 1820–70*, author Nina Baym points out that the authors of many traditional classics, and other celebrated books since, would "rather write about vapid angels and maligned temptresses than about what Louisa May Alcott called 'good, useful women'" and that the authors preferred "to present women as men's auxiliaries rather than center them in worlds of their own."

Asked how she would advise mothers in their selection of books for a mother-daughter book club, Nina suggests looking for women authors: "The very spectacle of the woman as a writer is very important to young girls. Sometimes it's the woman as a writer that's even more important than the character of a woman in the story.

"Read books by women. The very fact that a woman's name is on the book will mean something to a girl, even if it unspoken."

ELLEN SILBER

"Any story about a young woman or girl who has an inner life is a story that has a lot of possibilities," Nina says, "because one of the real pressures on girls is that they have to live for the outside world, for others. They're 'supposed to' listen and pick up on other people's thoughts, conform themselves, and not show much in the way of an inner life. So any books that show a thoughtful, responsive woman, even if she doesn't do exciting things, is good because it encourages women to listen to their own thinking, to say 'Yes, I have a mind and it's worth my while to explore my thoughts.'"

THE IMPORTANT THING
ABOUT THE BOOK IS...

Whatever books you choose, you want them to be enjoyable and thought-provoking for discussion. We also wanted to broaden our horizons as readers, so we looked for books the girls might not choose on their own.

We found that the novels that held up best under discussion

On Reading with Your Child

Reading aloud to a child, a parent can foster an introduction into a wonderful world of imagination in a way that doesn't happen in school because you're so much more focused on your own child, and can follow her, and your own, interests together.

One thing I think is important at the baseline of all of this is the intimacy somehow you can achieve by sharing literature, even before the question of discussion, the heightened experience you capture in literature makes it possible for people to get to a place closer to their heart, a place closer to the quick. Children feel this.

—ALICE LETVIN, PRESIDENT

The Great Books Foundation

READING THE CLASSICS: DEBUNKING MYTHS, GIVING GIRLS A VOICE

If you like the idea of reading classics, but you're put off by insensitive stereotypes, maddening views of girls and women, unsavory characters and brutal behavior, you're not alone. Here are some thoughts on fairy tales and how to talk through the hidden issues, from Ellen Silber, Ph.D., Director of the Marymount Institute for the Education of Women and Girls:

"I don't think children should read fairy tales unless they've got someone—an enlightened parent—to deconstruct the stories and show what's wrong. Someone who will ask:

"'What do you think about Snow White doing all the housework for the dwarfs? What do you think about Snow White in a coma and the prince coming along, and their getting married without ever having talked to each other about what's important to them? What do you think about all the bad older women in the fairy tales? What did the authors have against older women that they are there only as wicked witches, or other mean characters who persecute young girls? Why is that? What about the fact that Cinderella and Snow White do work that isn't very interesting, but they're patient, and they wait, and they get "the prize"— the handsome prince? And why is it always so important that they're pretty? Why is it a goal to get a man instead of to get a job, to get a life? Why do these women need rescuing? Is that the only way they can make it? Why are all the fairy tales so similar?'

"There are so many things you can say. If you don't say them, you're reinforcing the worst things those stories teach: passivity, hatred for other women, especially older women who in real life are so inventive and creative—none of the women get along together in these tales. That's such a lethal message.

"So, I think it's important for girls to read them, but not without someone to ask the really good questions."

Books to Grow On

I've focused on books for girls ages seven to twelve. Some of the books we've mentioned are serious, some are silly. Some are historical and some are contemporary. But what they have in common is that each is about a strong, smart girl who is a true hero in her own way. Naturally, we can't help mentioning the American Girls Collection stories, because Felicity, Kirsten, Addy, Samantha and Molly are all heroes to us!

The Hundred Dresses, Eleanor Estes
Julie of the Wolves, Jean Craighead George
From the Mixed-up Files of Mrs. Basil E. Frankweiler, E. L. Konigsburg
Prairie Songs, Pam Conrad
The Puppy Sister, S. E. Hinton

—JUDITH WOODBURN
Director of Editorial Development, Pleasant Company

were those that invited closer inspection. By that, I mean that the characters had some substance. They weren't simply good or bad, clever or dull, pretty or ugly. Their thoughts and choices made them interesting, even if they weren't always likable. The plots were engaging and unfolded in ways that weren't completely predictable. The author's language or style added to the richness of the reading experience, perhaps using words or phrases that could be understood in more than one way. There is no single right kind of book that does all those things. That's the beauty of books. Look around. Read around. Share what you find.

READING THE BOOK: SHARING TIME AND FEELINGS

When I remember reading as a little girl, it isn't necessarily the books I remember. It's the smell of the park where my mother would take us, picnic dinner in hand, for a luxurious evening stretched out on the grass, reading.

I've asked around, and everyone I know who enjoys reading as an adult—and even some who don't enjoy it all that much—has pleasant childhood memories of reading with someone special, or reading in a special place, or enjoy-

"Through the Mother-Daughter Book Club I have read many kinds of books and I found that they are all interesting in their own way."

ASHLEY S.

ing some special aspect of reading that often had nothing to do with the book. They remember parents or elderly aunts who read with them. They remember sitting under a tree in the backyard or in a quiet, out-of-the-way spot in their home. They remember flashlights and books under the covers. As much as we think of reading as a thing we *do*, I think that reading also is a thing we *feel*. It is an experience of the senses.

When we read with our children, we are more than narrators. We become partners in their experience of the book. We are their traveling companions as the story takes us 20,000 leagues under the sea, or through a terrifying escape from oppression to freedom through the underground railroad. Even more important, we're there for the moments of stories that reflect choices in life, choices that lead characters down one path or another.

Sometimes the stories inspire conversation about characters, their behavior or their choices, or perhaps about the places or people that are part of the landscape. But often, our reading just allows us to relax together. In those unhurried moments, Morgan sometimes tells me about something from her day, or shares a thought she's been tending until the coast was clear for quiet reflection.

Morgan is pretty protective of this time as "our" time and tries to discourage her older brother and younger sister from listening in. It doesn't always work out that way, and that's okay, too. Sometimes we read the book together; sometimes she wants to move ahead and I need to lag behind at my own pace.

Any way you devise your home reading routine is the right way if it works for you and your daughter. The mothers in our group each have a slightly different approach, and they change the routine when it needs to change.

Joyce includes both her daughters—Maya and her six-year-old sister—in the reading at bedtime.

Alice has made the home reading a family affair. It seemed that every time she sat down to read aloud with her daughter in the family room, the others just quietly gravitated over. "It's amazing," she says, "but when I read aloud, all my children all come around. It's become a family thing—a time for all of us to come together."

Kathie and Jihan have a routine that includes a little bit of everything: "Sometimes I read to her, and sometimes she reads to me, and sometimes we read separately and come back and talk about it together," Kathie says. "It means we always have something in particular to talk about."

In addition to the pure pleasure of reading with our girls and talking with them as we progress through a story, we've also

FICTIONAL CHARACTERS: LEARNING FROM THE BEST AND THE WORST

The learning experience in a book is in the discussion much more than in any message you or I think the books are sending. It's the conversation that turns out to be more important.

You can have a very negative character, but it can serve as a stimulus for girls or young women to make connections. A character we think is wonderful might look priggish to a girl today. I wouldn't want to censor the characters of the books we give to our girls, but I would want to stress the importance of a woman author.

There may be the feeling that old books aren't germane, but I think it's good to read old books. There's no guarantee the book will be the same book for the next generation. The mothers may learn as much as the daughters. I wouldn't say to teach every book you loved as a child, but some of them have a lot of staying power.

—NINA BAYM, AUTHOR
Woman's Fiction: A Guide to Novels by and about Women in America, 1820–70

Books to Grow On

Six books I'd really want my teenaged daughter to read

(if I had one):

Shizuko's Daughter, Kyoko Mori

Celine, Brock Cole

Weetzie Bat, Francesca L. Block

Gift from the Sea, Anne Morrow Lindbergh

High Wind in Jamaica, Richard Hughes

Letters to a Young Poet, Rainer Maria Rilke

The Trials of Molly Sheldon, Julian F. Thompson

—JULIAN F. THOMPSON, AUTHOR
The Fling

discovered that our involvement supports their growth as readers and critical thinkers. Each of our girls has her own strengths and challenges along those lines—all of us do, in fact. By reading together, each mother has been able to tailor the home reading approach to meet her own daughter's individual needs or wishes.

For instance:

✶ When the girls read aloud, we're able to identify when they have trouble with pronunciation, which also may mean they aren't familiar with the word. Sometimes they'll stop and ask about a word. If they appear to be struggling with it, or skipping past it, we might guide them through sounding it out and add a quick explanation of the word.

✶ When the mothers read, the girls become engrossed as listeners and tend to comment or ask questions more often about the story.

✶ Before we read, we might ask our daughter to refresh our memory about where we were in the story. This retelling process develops her ability to organize her thoughts and focus on main ideas.

✶ A character's behavior or other action in the story may prompt one of us to bring up a similar moment or experience from our own lives. It really does happen, and it makes for some very special moments!

Even if you each read independently, you can compare notes on the story as you progress, encourage the retelling and reflection and share each other's reactions to the story. In her comments, you can listen for any hints that your daughter might need some additional support from you in reading or understanding the story.

Pam at the Cheshire Cat Bookstore points out that sometimes the first few chapters of a book, or a chapter introducing a new character, may seem formidable to a young reader. They may need some help getting into the book.

"Certain chapters are like meeting somebody for the first time—you may be a little uncomfortable—and you've got to get beyond that," Pam says. "Especially if it's not very fast-paced, it's useful to sit and read that chapter together and help them get beyond that. Once they do, you'd be amazed at what starts happening."

"What starts happening" is really the essence of the Mother-Daughter Book Club. We read more, we share more and we enjoy more.

ACTIVE READERS—DON'T JUST READ!

The Great Books Foundation, in its leader training materials, describes the "interpretive reader" as one who "reads actively, raising questions and striving for understanding. An interpretive reader wants to know why the characters in the story act as they do, what the meaning might be of unusual or surprising events—what an author is trying to communicate through his or her words."

Whatever you call it, active reading is rewarding.

Here are some fun tips to turn on the active reader in your life—*just don't use them all at once!*

✳ **Express surprise or wonder** at a character's actions and ask why the character might have done what she or he did.

✳ **Wonder aloud** about how things might have turned out if something had happened differently, if a character had made a different choice or if people had responded differently at a certain point in the story. Ask your daughter how the story might have unfolded differently or ended differently.

✳ **Ask your daughter** how she would like the story to end, or how she might have made it end if she were the writer.

✳ **Mark words, phrases, ideas** or anything you think might make a good question for discussion. Encourage your daughter to do the same.

★ **Pick at some details.** Why might the author have used certain words or images? What was she or he trying to convey? Did it work?

★ **Play with words.** Some words or phrases can be understood in more than one way. How does it change the story if the word or phrase is understood differently?

★ **Just for fun:** Invite your daughter on a "scavenger hunt" for five new or unusual vocabulary words or phrases from the text to share with the group.

> *"Don't make your books childish, because if you read babyish books, some of the older girls won't enjoy them."*
>
> BRITTNEY

★ **Compare art to life:** How do your real-life experiences or your observations compare to what you read in the book?

MOTHERS AS GATEKEEPERS: CALLING ALL IDEAS, INSPIRATION

I enjoy the search for "good books." I like hunting up authors and stories we may not have encountered before, I like reading the books to preview them for the group, and I enjoy the excitement of finding the gems to introduce to our club, books we would otherwise have overlooked. I also believe that any mother who is willing to help organize a book discussion group very likely wants to use it to expose her daughter to the shelves of fine literature that the girls might not get around to reading in school or on their own.

That said, I think it's important to add that it's hard to go very wrong with as many well-written books as there are today—from classics to modern fiction, biographies and poetry—and with a group of mothers and daughters who like to talk about stories, ideas and feelings. Give yourselves some credit: If a book turns out to be a little thin, it won't sustain much discussion on its

POETRY: READING INTO
THE WORLD OF EMOTIONS

Mothers have a gorgeous opportunity to introduce their daughters to poetry. Especially as girls grow older and outgrow the rhyme-scheme poetry so frequently used with younger children, they can enjoy free verse poetry—so flexible and full of images and ideas. Poems about nature, animals, people—these are wonderful for getting kids to respond. Poetry is the most immediate form of expression of feelings. Of all kinds of writing, it speaks most directly to the human heart. Poetry makes feelings very accessible—the perfect source for a mother-daughter discussion!

Some questions that will take a discussion into the heart of a poem might be:

* **What is the poem about?**

* **What is the poet saying,** what are the words saying?

* **Can you sense any feelings** the poet might have about the topic? Look in words, lines, phrases.

* **Do you feel** there are any hidden meanings?

* **Where might the poet be writing?** Outside under a tree? Inside, in a pleasant place, or from a lonely window seat?

* **Have you ever felt like this?** Have you ever looked at a tree or a flower or an animal and said, "Yes, that's how I feel!"

* **Could you identify** the person writing?

* **Have you ever written** about this topic?

—JOAN FRANKLIN SMUTNY, EDUCATOR, AUTHOR

merits, but in discussion you can reflect on the quality of the story and the writing, what they give the reader and what they don't.

The fact is, even if you read a 1930s Nancy Drew mystery book, there are ways to talk about characters and plot, attitudes and expectations that reflect the era in which they were written.

The girls are learning all the time; the mother-daughter dialogue thrives.

I've been reminded of the value of *all reading* as I've heard or read reflections by respected authors, scholars and others who speak of it, and sometimes of their own memories of reading.

Virginia Hamilton, celebrated author of so many fine books, recalls her early reading with a laugh:

"When I was young I read a great deal—I had sisters and they brought books into the house—and I loved the Nancy Drew stories. Some librarians don't like it when I say that, but those books were very available and I found Nancy Drew very interesting. She had her own car and she solved mysteries!"

When we think about age and reading levels, we should try to be less concerned about matching numbers and screening out things we're "not sure they're ready for" and more open to the challenge—and potential inspiration—of stretching ahead, notes Rita Dove, 1966 U.S. Poet Laureate:

"It's a real danger, you know, making children's books too easy, presenting lessons in them instantly and effortlessly.... It's such a danger, because nothing in life that is worth anything is presented instantly to us, and children are perfectly willing to be challenged by something."

Stretching to meet new ideas, to reflect upon them and to discuss them, is the work of life and the heart of what we want to share with our daughters.

Jane Addams, social activist and 1931 Nobel Peace Prize winner, said it clearly, nearly a hundred years ago in the book *Twenty Years at Hull House.*

"Perhaps I may record here my protest against the efforts, so often made, to shield children and young people from all that has to do with death and sorrow, to give them a good time at all hazards on the assumption that the ills of life will come soon enough. Young people themselves often resent this attitude on the part of their elders; they feel set aside and belittled as if they were denied the common human experiences."

And our bookstore friend Pam Sacks brings that thought to us as it relates to our mother-daughter discussions today and into the future. "You can't rewrite history but you *can* discuss it," Pam says. "If you read a book where the moms feel girls are treated in an old-fashioned way, then discuss it. Ask them to compare it to how things are today—or how they would want them to be."

> *"Now when I read a book I think it through, and sometimes I go back and read a page again and again."*
>
> MAYA

Whatever book you read with your daughter, whatever book you discuss within your club, it is transformed by the sharing. So are we all.

ENDNOTES

✱ Make sure someone you know and trust has read a book before you recommend it to the club.

✱ Be creative—novels aren't the only kinds of books.

✱ Choose books that are both enjoyable and thought-provoking.

CHAPTER FIVE

HOW TO STRUCTURE AND LEAD GROUPS

The most important thing about being a leader

is to have good questions and let everybody give their answers.

— MORGAN

JIHAN AND KATHIE THOMPSON

Hi! I am Jihan Thompson and I am twelve years old, in sixth grade at National Cathedral School. I love to horseback ride, read and write. I am basically always happy, and I have a cheerful disposition toward everything I do. I am a very willing, carefree person. I love to laugh and I love to make other people laugh. I love to be happy. My hobby is collecting postcards, and at this time I have fifty different ones from around the world. The quality I like most about myself is that I am very happy.

My mom is Kathie Elaine Clark Thompson, and she is a hearing and speech therapist at many different schools in the Washington, D.C. area. She is tall and has light brown hair. My mom is also a happy person. She has a positive and cheerful disposition toward everything and everyone. She is a very cheerful and understanding person. The qualities I like best about my mom are that she is happy and she makes me laugh.

My mother and I are very close, and I think that the Mother-Daughter Book Club has brought us even closer together. The book club also has given my mom and me something to talk about. These are a few of the many reasons I love the book club.

Another reason is I have been able to meet other friendly girls outside of school. The book club has introduced me to a fantastic assortment of books that I probably would not have read before. I also have been given the experience of reading books about girls from different cultures. At one of our book club meetings we got to meet the author and see a film on one of the books we read —*The Friends* by Rosa Guy.

One of the best things I like about our club is that I get to read a book and share my views with other people and maybe discuss my feelings about the book. I like to be able to share my opinion. I like doing it in our club because with the other books I read, I really cannot share my opinions or feelings because I have no one to share them with. I think the book club has broadened my horizons to new and different things. My favorite book that we read in the club was *Charlie Pippin*.

One of the best stories that has unfolded within our circle wasn't on our book list at all. It's been the story of our own daughters growing up and, one by one, meeting by meeting, showing maturing qualities of friendship, intelligence and leadership, all in the space of a two-hour book club session. This doesn't happen by accident. But it's not something anyone can put on an agenda.

In fact, the philosophy that shapes our club's structure and leadership style reflects the reality of our lives as girls and women. All of us, whatever our ages, have a need for friendship and laughter, for the stimulation that reading and discussion bring to our lives, and for the opportunity to grow within this special and supportive circle. Just as we're making the time and space in our lives for the Mother-Daughter Book Club, the way we structure our time together makes it meaningful, comfortable and rewarding. Our club creates a time and space for us to *be*.

> *"A woman might be prepared to give some complicated analysis, and a girl might simply say, 'I thought it was great.' Well, how do we talk from there? You can say—and it's better if you're not the one saying it to your own daughter—'I thought this scene was really strange' or 'I don't understand why a girl would do that, can we act it out...' and often that can be a fun way to ask those questions."*
>
> ELIZABETH DEBOLD

Once you focus on the meeting structure as a reflection of your group—not a management device—the rest falls into place. For example, when we arrive for a meeting, the girls head off one way to socialize while the mothers meet separately to take care of any administrative details, to preview books and unwind a bit.

We didn't set it up that way; it just happened the first time we met and it felt right. It worked for everybody. And it still does. That little socializing up front gives the girls time to *play*, time to connect with one another before they widen their circle to connect with us.

Tips for Structuring Meetings and Leadership

* **Keep it simple.**

* **Avoid written agendas,** assignment sheets or anything that looks or sounds like school or homework.

* **Encourage the girls** to take charge of the club and let each one exercise her judgment in her own way. Encourage creativity *and* simplicity in hosting and planning any book-related activity. (See Chapter Ten: "Beyond the Books.")

* **When in doubt,** err on the side of respecting the girls' choices. If the selection process is open to any books the girls suggest, then be ready to start sleuthing if they choose a Nancy Drew mystery.

* **Instead of rigid rules,** express expectations: respect for each other during discussion, and commitment to the club in terms of reading the books, attending meetings and contributing to discussion. If you're going to be absent for a meeting, let the host know.

* **Decide how you feel about absences** or attendance of girls without their moms. Although we all understand that a twosome is preferred, on the occasional afternoon when either mother or daughter simply can't come, we encourage the other to come alone. Sometimes it becomes clear that a mother and daughter simply can't attend depend-

ably. Then give them a graceful way out. Most likely you'll continue to see them and value them as friends—so show you respect their priorities and wish them well.

   ✱ **Encourage the open expression of ideas and feelings.** Unlike most adult book discussion groups, where sharing related tales or feelings is discouraged, the Mother-Daughter Book Club is just the place for that kind of sharing, along with more objective responses in discussing stories or characters.

   ✱ **Set a good example.** When the girls hear us sharing thoughts—including different points of view—in a respectful, collaborative way, they're learning about the world of women in a way they won't see in many TV sitcoms, movies or even books.

   ✱ **Don't feel pressured** to demonstrate smart, witty, insightful, sophisticated and sensitive literary analysis. Relax, listen, contribute when it's comfortable and watch for ways to help the girls explore the questions they seem to find compelling.

   ✱ **In all matters, ask instead of tell,** and facilitate only when the girls make it clear they need help.

The sound effects for those thirty minutes—giggles, squeals, easy laughter and confident camaraderie—remind me each time that our girls are at a special age of in between. They still have this wonderful, silly energy that they're quick to lavish all over one another. Then a few minutes later, they're debating fine points of character development in a novel. As a mother, you wonder: How can they seem so young one minute and so much older the next? The answer is, they *are* young, and everything they are is part of that. They still have a need to giggle and play. They also have a need to exercise their intellect and leadership abilities in an environment of support and good times.

Another aspect of the meeting that has become established over time is the uninterupted forty-five minutes we reserve for our discussion period. Once everyone's had a chance to relax and socialize for that initial half hour or so, we call the girls back and gather around for the discussion.

"Even though children may not show you they've changed their mind, once they savor the conversation—it may be weeks or years from now—they'll think about it and understand and maybe at some point say, 'Ah, I see what my mother was saying, now I understand.'"

ALEXIS CHRISTIAN

Forty-five minutes might seem like a long time, but both the girls and the moms feel it's just right. It's long enough for some real back-and-forth among the girls and mothers, long enough to explore ideas, to follow up on comments that beg for it, long enough for us all to enjoy expressing our thoughts in an unhurried way.

"We have different perspectives," Alexis says, "and one person will interpret something differently from another. It's been fascinating to hear my daughter express herself and get a read on her in this way. The group dynamics are wonderful."

We hold off on refreshments until *after* the discussion, enjoying that as another opportunity for relaxed socializing. If your mother-daughter book club meets after school, you may want to put refreshments out for the girls' arrival time. That gives them an energy boost for the discussion period, and puts a comfortable distance between snack and dinnertime. Whether the food comes before or after, it's nice to not have it as a distraction *during* discussion. The ups and downs for refills, and inevitable questions about who wants what, can sidetrack discussion.

Over time, you'll find that different mothers and daughters will contribute their talents in special ways. For instance, Alice, in our group, volunteered to write a simple one-page "newsletter" or update for our members. It includes some highlights from our last meeting's discussion, and any other information or reminders we want to circulate. It's been especially helpful for those who miss a meeting. And even if you were there, it's fun to read!

Every mother-daughter book club is unique and needs a structure that reflects the group's personality and objectives. If you all agree on some basic principles from the beginning, including hosting duties and a hosting and meeting schedule, then the leader simply keeps the group on track by tending to the other "light housekeeping" of administrative detail.

TIPS FOR THE CLUB LEADER

If your group plans a few meetings at a time instead of a year's worth, let the mothers know when they'll need to be prepared to plan some dates at the next meeting. Be the calendar watchdog.

If an author appearance or community event is of special interest to your group, bring it up for discussion. Stay active in the book and author hunt and encourage the other mothers and daughters to do the same.

"I like the fact that the girls are so invested in this. They do look forward to it, even with the workload they have at school and after school, they won't give it up."

KATHIE THOMPSON

You may want to ask one mother each time to handle the book-buying task, and let the others pick up their books from her and reimburse her for the expense. Or it may be more practical for each mother and daughter to be responsible for getting their own copies of the selection. Consider asking a local bookstore to provide your mother-daughter book club with a discount in exchange for buying multiple copies of the book.

New Faces, New Friends: New Members and Guests

Don't forget to put out the welcome mat for guests to your mother-daughter book club from time to time. Invite the grandmothers or aunts to read a book with you and join you for discussion. The girls might like to invite a special teacher from school. Or you may want to invite a respected person in the community whose area of expertise or activism ties in to the theme of your book. Guests add another vibrant perspective to the mix, and the girls experience the benefits of meeting and discussing ideas with someone they might not otherwise hear.

New members are another consideration. It's hard to imagine any group going on for any length of time without losing members to job transfers or other schedule priorities. The Mother-Daughter Book Club is no different. While it might seem tempting to invite mother-daughter guests to attend as prospective members, our group has tried to avoid any situation that leads to talking about other mothers or daughters who are not present, or "judging" guests for an invitation to join the group.

I'd suggest that when you feel the membership of your group has dropped to the point of needing some new regulars, you review your group's focus and any other relevant considerations, then think the prospects through in the same way you did to start your group. Someone will need to take responsibility—"take the heat"—for choosing whom to invite. Poll the mothers for any suggestions—they can ask their daughters for suggestions at home—and invite your "new member."

BOOKS TO GROW ON

I naturally consulted my daughter, Molly, who at age sixteen is one of the wisest readers I know. We both made up lists, put them together and agonized over paring our choices down to a few, but agreed that the six titles we came up with—all coming-of-age stories, set in different times and places—were books we cared passionately about, books we would read and reread always. Here they are in no particular order:

A Tree Grows in Brooklyn, Betty Smith
Rumors of Peace, Ella Leffland
Anne of Green Gables, Lucy M. Montgomery
The Country Girls Trilogy and Epilogue, Edna O'Brien
To Kill a Mockingbird, Harper Lee
Anne Frank: The Diary of a Young Girl, Anne Frank

—SUZANNE FREEMAN, AUTHOR
The Cuckoo's Child

GUIDANCE VS. INDEPENDENCE:
STRUCTURING TOGETHERNESS
FOR GROWTH

Bertha Waters, a parent-training consultant, licensed social worker, mother of seven (including five daughters!), also serves on the Federal Advisory Commission of the Mary McLeod Bethune Council House National Historic Site. Ms. Waters' daughters—all busy women now—sometimes join her as copresenters in her programs on women's history, health and life relationships.

Asked how mothers can strengthen the mother-daughter bond yet respect their need for independence, she shared this story from her own life, about a moment when reading and mothering came together for a special and lasting result:

"Years ago, when I was a young mother, I read a magazine article about a very respected mother, and someone asked her her secret. She said: 'Don't nag them; let them be as much as possible.'

"I had three children at that time. In those days—this was in the 1950s—it was considered out of style to have more than two children, so when we'd ride the trolley I'd always be right on them for every move they made or word they said, trying to make them behave perfectly—better than perfect—so no one would give us those disapproving looks.

"Well, with that mother's words in mind, I decided that when I rode the trolley I would sit in one seat and read—which I loved to do and never had enough time for—and I'd let my children sit in the seat behind me and I wouldn't get involved in what they were doing or saying unless they got to a point where it interrupted my reading. Everything worked out fine! And I remember that as a turning point for me, when I chose to be a person, and stopped being a 'professional mother,' and let them *be*."

TIPS FOR THE HOSTING MOTHER AND DAUGHTER

It's helpful to send out reminders a week or so before you host the mother-daughter book club meeting. Include the date, time and place of the next meeting and the name of the book.

Remember, discussion is the main course at the meetings. Don't feel pressured to put out fancy food. For fun, look to the book: sometimes the story includes a recipe or description of foods that you might make for the group.

The hosting daughter usually serves as leader for the discussion. She prepares questions to get the discussion started and keep it going along lines that interested her as she read the book. (See Chapter Six: "Discussion.") The host mom also may plan to bring up points for discussion.

If you want to try a book-related activity, it may include something as simple as bringing out a globe to locate geographic points of interest in a story or making refreshments that reflect the ethnic cuisine, as Linda and Rebecca did when they hosted the discussion for *Charlie Pippin*, a story with a tie to Vietnam. Your daughter might devise a game format for the discussion period, or you might arrange to visit an exhibit or see a film that relates to the book, and have discussion there or over dessert afterward. It's important to keep this optional, and remember that you really need no more than the book and the group to have a great discussion. (See Chapter Ten: "Beyond the Books.")

"Thou shalt not correct to the point of causing frustration. Thou shalt not show any negative reaction to anything that is said, or make fun of anything that is said."

GRACE S.

A PLACE TO SPEAK FREELY AND GROW

How do you both let go and stay connected to your daughter? No textbook can show you the way. You just have to live it, listen to others who have been through it, and on occasion, step back and understand what's really behind the issue of the moment.

Underneath the yelling and screaming about "Help me with homework," there's a more profound statement being made: "I want to do it on my own. I want you there, but I don't want you there."

I think what happens during the middle school years is the struggle for identity: "Who am I? Who do I want to be? What is it about my mother I like? What is it I don't like?" That fuels a lot of the struggle that sometimes occurs between mothers and daughters.

Whether they know it or not, when our daughters look in the mirror they look at us. Perhaps they don't always like what they see when they see what they may become. But they can't escape it. They'll come to either embrace it or reject it at times, and therein lies part of the struggle at this stage of their lives. They don't have what I have at fifty—or even at twenty-seven—a larger experience base and a broader view of what this relationship really is all about.

So many women I talk to who have grown daughters say they struggled during certain phases of their daughters' adolescence, and the relationships emerged totally transformed as their daughters became young adults. But you are not a young adult when you're thirteen.

—WHITNEY RANSOME
National Coalition of Girls' Schools

ONWARD AND ONWARD:
THE CLUB'S STORY UNFOLDS

It's easy to get distracted by all the exciting possibilities when you get good books and enthusiastic girls and women together. I like to encourage creativity, using simplicity as a touchstone. The best investment any of us can make in preparing for a meeting is simply to *read the book* with our daughters, enjoy talking about it together some at home, plan some thought-provoking questions and come ready to share our thoughts. That thoughtful time and sharing with our daughters is the best investment we can make, period.

ENDNOTES

✳ Keep it simple.

✳ Encourage the girls to be creative and take charge of hosting and planning group activities.

✳ Prepare questions in advance, but welcome impromptu digressions that interest the group.

✳ Invite guests for special meetings or even new members to enliven the circle.

CHAPTER SIX

DISCUSSION

The learning experience in a book is in the discussion

much more than in any message you or I think the books are sending.

It's the conversation that turns out to be more important.

—NINA BAYM

Holly & Alice Lacey Thomas

Hello, my name is Holly N'neka Thomas and I'm ten years old.
I'm in fourth grade and I'm one of the youngest members of the Mother-Daughter Book Club.

I'm a Junior Girl Scout, and I take ballet, piano and violin. I like to play piano, but I don't take lessons from a regular teacher. My cousin knows how to play very well and is teaching me. I have a canary named Sweety, and I want a black horse real bad.

I like to ride my bike, and I like to wear jeans. My favorite clothes are my black jeans and my velvet long-sleeved shirt. Usually when I get dressed up to go out I wear a dress, but I'd rather stay home.

One of my favorite places to be is Mickey's house—Mickey is a little dog who lives a little way away from my house, around the corner and all the way down. There are about fifteen dogs in my neighborhood, but he's my favorite. He's small and fluffy and growls at other people, but not at me.

My mother's name is Alice Lacey Thomas. She works at home, being a mom, taking care of me, my brother Trevor, who is twelve, my sister Meghan, who is fifteen, and my dad. She used to write things for big companies, and then she wrote some children's books with my dad—he's the minister at our church—but they haven't published the books yet. She has good ideas. My mom and I like to cook together and go to the movies.

We like to read the books for the Mother-Daughter Book Club together. I like reading on my own all right, but I like it best when my mom reads to me. My mom reads a lot of other books, too. *The Thorn Birds* is her favorite book—she's read it every year for fifteen years!

My favorite book from the club is *The Ear, the Eye and the Arm*.

I don't know whether it's a gender thing or just a sign of intelligent life, but when girls get together they talk. They like to talk about things they like and about things they don't like. They'll debate about anything, *anything*, until they lose interest, and then they'll drop it so fast you can hear it thud.

When I overhear a conversation between girls at the museum or on a playground, or listen to Morgan relaxed and chatting with her friends, I am impressed by the passion they invest in expressing themselves. Whether they're negotiating turns on the swings or bemoaning a homework assignment, they do it with feeling and they do a thorough job. If you can get past the *sound* of it—the part we tend to call whining or complaining—and listen for the *structure*, you'll often hear all the makings of mature, intelligent discussion: A girl states her case, expresses her opinion, backs it up with some evidence, entertains other views and eventually arrives at a conclusion that ends the conversation.

> *"I like to use the sleight of hand: You think a character is one thing and then it turns out the character is more than you thought."*
>
> VIRGINIA HAMILTON

So, how do you tap into that reservoir of conversational energy and funnel it into a satisfying group discussion of literature and life?

There are some time-honored approaches that are helpful, such as the "shared inquiry" method of the Great Books Foundation, and other guidelines put forth by book club experts such as the American Library Association. As helpful as the guidelines are, it's important to remember that they're written for groups that come together to focus on the literature—*not* on the personal lives of the readers.

The Mother-Daughter Book Club is unique in our desire to explore literature *and* strengthen our mother-daughter relationships through the shared experience of reading, discussion and reflection that very much includes our personal lives. Not only that, but our goal is for the *girls to lead discussion*—not the mothers.

The discussion simply won't sound like a college literature class or any book discussion group with an adult leader. But when, over the course of a few meetings, you start to see your daughter expressing herself confidently, asking thought-provoking questions, listening carefully to others and encouraging others to speak and be heard, the sound of that discussion is a joyful noise.

If we want our girls to learn about leadership, we have to step back from the role of expert more often and let them practice it. The Mother-Daughter Book Club is the perfect place for it. They are among caring friends and loving mothers. No family politics, no grades or evaluations, no fear of failure, no risk of shame. Just happy opportunity.

> *"A big part of how I learned to be a woman was overhearing my mother talk with her woman friends, watching how grown women talk to each other."*
>
> ELIZABETH WHEELER,
> *Assistant Professor of English,*
> *University of Oregon*

So, as you read advice here or anywhere on how to lead discussion, when it comes to "rules" of discussion, remember that the first rule—and maybe the only rule—of the Mother-Daughter Book Club is that you always do what's comfortable and what works for you and your particular group of girls and mothers. Structure dictates so much of life outside this special circle; let your daughters lead the way here. You'll like where they take you.

DISCUSSION: SHINING A LIGHT INTO THE HEART OF THINGS

When I think of our Mother-Daughter Book Club's most enjoyable and satisfying discussions, the quality that best describes them is illuminating. A good book tells a story. A good book discussion illuminates that story with the light of experience each of us brings to it. Discussion also adds to our experience of the book and of one another. We see farther, deeper or from a different perspective. It can be transforming.

One example stands out in my mind:

Patty Ann was the girl everyone loved to hate. One of the key characters in the book *Cousins*, by Virginia Hamilton, Patty Ann is beautiful, talented, always well dressed, and earns the best grades in school. She also is a snob and her mother is, too. Did I leave anything out?

Patty Ann's disgruntled cousin Cammy echoes our own daughters' sentiments when she describes Patty Ann as so "good at everything...in school, at home, at her piano [that] everything she did was like chalk scraping on a blackboard." By the time the story plays out to its dramatic conclusion, Patty Ann doesn't have any sympathizers—in the book or among the Mother-Daughter Book Club girls.

In our discussion of *Cousins*, the story's plot and action grabbed everyone's immediate attention. But as we began to question the details of one critical episode, our discussion moved back to Patty Ann and her attitude: that impervious diamond-like perfection that put everyone off so.

One comment led to another, and scouring the text for clues, we talked our way back, *past* Patty Ann's facade of perfection, to a place where we could look more objectively at her. Once there, we discovered that in many ways her world reflected the real world we all know well, where pressures for perfection are all around, and where girls measure themselves constantly against one standard or another.

> ## BOOKS TO GROW ON
>
> The King James Version of the Bible
>
> *Catcher in the Rye,*
> J. D. Salinger
>
> *Jane Eyre,*
> Charlotte Brontë
>
> *Wuthering Heights,*
> Emily Brontë
>
> *David Copperfield,*
> Charles Dickens
>
> —KAYE GIBBONS, AUTHOR
> *Ellen Foster*

Comments from mothers and daughters showed a surprising difference in how we each perceived the Patty Ann character and her motives. And the perceptions weren't divided along generational lines. Some girls thought she shouldn't have been so stuck up. Others didn't like her, but thought her attitude was understandable given the fact that she was, in fact, smart, pretty and talented. Some mothers remembered a girl like Patty Ann from their childhoods; others remembered *being* Patty Ann, at least in some ways, as a bright, talented girl who didn't fit in, or feeling a relentless pressure to excel at everything they did.

By the end of the discussion, Patty Ann wasn't the snooty stranger she had been an hour before. The story felt closer—as if we'd *been* there. And the feelings we had shared made each of us more *visible* to the other, more real as an individual with life experience and a point of view, no matter what our age.

"In books, you're talking about experience and life a little removed, so you have a wonderful vehicle for people to talk about themselves, in addition to learning about someone else's vision. And you can try on other visions, the many different portraits of girls and women."

ELLEN SILBER

"Discussing issues in the group is different than reading alone or discussing it just the two of us at home," Alexis says. "There's an added benefit. Not only do I hear myself and my daughter talk, but she hears the other mothers, as do I, and where I might hold back saying something, some other mothers will go ahead and say it, and I can get my daughter's opinion—my daughter can agree or disagree and it's just part of the group discussion—not a personal issue with me. And it's wonderful because we come from such varied backgrounds that we all bring something different to the group."

The death of a baby in another story we read was heartfelt by the mothers in our group. When none of the girls picked up on that as a point for discussion, we asked them what they thought of it. The truth was, they didn't much. One of the girls volunteered that she'd feel sad about it. Another said she'd feel sad, but then get on with things. There was, of course, no way they could imagine the loss in the way a mother would. Some of us described what we were feeling about it, and how the loss might have affected the characters within the context of the story. And

Books to Grow On

BOOKS:

Aesop's Fables

Greek Myths, Geraldine McCaughrean

Grimms' Fairy Tales, Jacob and Wilhelm Grimm

Hans Christian Andersen's Fairy Tales, Hans Christian Andersen

Alice's Adventures in Wonderland, Lewis Carroll

Lord of the Flies, William Golding

POETRY:

The Rime of the Ancient Mariner, Samuel Taylor Coleridge

Shakespeare's Sonnets, William Shakespeare

Sonnets from the Portuguese, Elizabeth Barrett Browning

Invictus, William Ernest Henley

"A Psalm of Life," Henry Wadsworth Longfellow

"In Memory of W. B. Yeats," W. H. Auden

Annabel Lee, Edgar Allan Poe

—DIANE RAVITCH, HISTORIAN OF EDUCATION
New York University

then—in the words of our young partners—we got on with things.

"If we get a reaction, that's wonderful," Grace says. "If we don't, then we just move on. We don't want the point to get ignored, but we don't harp on it."

GIRLS REACT TO WHAT WE SAY— AND DON'T SAY

When a subject hits a dead end, it may signal a lack of interest or it may be because the girls are taking a detour because they sense a roadblock up ahead.

Elizabeth Debold, a developmental psychologist and co-author of *Mother Daughter Revolution: From Good Girls to Great Women*, suggests that the obstacle to discussion sometimes is an unspoken dialogue that often goes on between mothers and daughters:

"Girls are also incredibly sensitive to who we are and what we expect as mothers, and where our anxieties are. Sometimes if we are really prepared to talk about a 'big issue' and are nervous about it, girls have a profound instinct about wanting to stay away from that. They'll turn away from the discussion because they feel there's something bothering their mom."

If we can say what we feel—sad, confused, angry—instead of silencing ourselves about things that disturb us, it gives our daughters an opportunity to know us as people—which is what they want. Then we open the possibility for true dialogue and connection.

"If you listen to the kinds of comments girls make about these things, they don't say, 'the character development was really poor,' or, 'I had trouble believing the plot.' They may say it felt fake or tell you they thought one of the characters was dumb—developmentally they're at a very different place than you are," Elizabeth Debold says. "But if you listen to them speak, in their own terms, you can hear that they're seriously engaged."

DISCUSSIONS THAT WORK:
STRATEGIES FOR SUCCESS

Not every book inspires soulful reflections. Some discussions are more memorable than others. Some are memorable more for their humor, unexpected reactions or a sudden encounter of a generation or maturity gap. All of them can be satisfying in one way or another.

A lively discussion needs a sense of purpose or direction, good questions, enthusiastic participation, recognition of each person's contribution and a satisfying conclusion. Most of that boils down to thoughtful reading, careful reflection and a respectful leadership style by girls and mothers.

"Some girls talk more than others and it's good when the quiet ones talk, too," Jamexis says. "It's more fun for them because then they're not just sitting there. And then everybody gets to hear their ideas."

"Don't ask questions where the answer's too easy or right there in front of you," Brittney suggests. "It's more fun if it's an answer you have to look up or think about."

One of the most helpful guides to leading discussion is *An Introduction to Shared Inquiry*, a reader-friendly training manual by the Great Books Foundation. "Great Books," as most people call the foundation, has provided materials and training for book discussion groups across the United States for many years. The Great

> ## BOOKS TO GROW ON
>
> Fiction about women coming of age in hard times:
>
> *How the Garcia Girls Lost Their Accents*,
> Julia Alvarez
>
> *Jane Eyre*,
> Charlotte Brontë
>
> *The Grass Is Singing*,
> Doris Lessing
>
> *The Joy Luck Club*,
> Amy Tan
>
> *Jasmine*,
> Bharati Mukherjee
>
> *The Beet Queen*,
> Louise Erdrich
>
> — KATHLEEN COURRIER,
> PUBLICATIONS DIRECTOR
> World Resources Institute

QUESTIONS: IT TAKES ALL KINDS

✶ **Questions of fact** help define the story. Use these to make sure the girls understand what happened factually. Questions of fact can lead us back to the text to see what the author said, compared to what we thought the author said.

✶ **Questions of interpretation** have several different answers that can be supported with evidence from the text. Why *did* a character do it, why *would* a character do it?

✶ **Questions of evaluation** ask us to think about something in the work in light of our own knowledge, values or life experience. To decide whether we agree or disagree with the author's idea or point of view. What does the author say? What does the author mean? Do I agree with it?

— *Adapted from* An Introduction to Shared Inquiry, *Third Edition,*
The Great Books Foundation

Books style, as described in the leader's manual, offers a carefully structured approach to group discussion that focuses intently upon "fundamental questions raised by the text."

"The search is inherently active," the Great Books manual notes, because "it involves taking what the author has given us and trying to grasp its full meaning, to interpret or reach an understanding of the text in light of our experience and using sound reasoning."

One mother in our group is a trained Junior Great Books discussion leader, and we have all benefited from the wisdom she brings from Great Books and her experience with groups of children using the program. We've borrowed from that sense of structure, creating our own unique approach to combine active reading, critical thinking and the relaxed interaction of mothers, daughters and friendship.

The results are worthwhile.

"In the school setting my daughter was becoming a little reserved, but in our club discussions, I can actually hear her thoughts, and she's much more expressive," says Alexis. "I watch her as she listens to others, and she has become much more in-depth in the way she asks questions and listens to the answers. I can see she's really trying to understand someone else's point of view."

TO GET A GOOD ANSWER, ASK A GOOD QUESTION

Spirited discussions begin with strong questions. Strong questions come in a lot of shapes and sizes, but what they have in common is that they lead through a process of discovery.

In the early meetings of our Mother-Daughter Book Club, the girls often came up with questions like those you might imagine on a fill-in-the-blank test at school. "What game did Jimmy hate to play?" "How did the wolf mother feed her babies?" The questions went for facts but didn't ask for much in the way of reflection or analysis. The girls had fun with them, regardless, but the mothers felt obliged to toss out follow-up questions that probed a little more deeply: "*Why* did Jimmy hate to play baseball?" And if he hated it so much, "*Why did he continue to play it?*"

With each daughter's hosting experience and her questions to lead discussion, all the girls learned a little more about what kinds of questions seemed to spark discussion.

Then one day a reporter called and wanted to sit in on a meeting and write about our club. Our next meeting was weeks away and they wanted the story *now*. We weren't ready to discuss our next book, so we called a special meeting, and came prepared with questions that had us compare characters, plots and other aspects of the first three or four books we had read. It was a *wonderful* discussion. This single experience of comparing and contrasting from book to book gave the girls a model for using comparison as a way to think and talk about literature.

"I'm not so sure that any one particular type of character in a book is good or bad. What is much more important is for the character to be talked about—to hear this opinion and that opinion and get different perspectives on the character."

NINA BAYM

Since that time, the girls routinely bring in questions that include comparisons from book to book. And our discussions weave and reweave previous themes and characters into the material of the moment. That frame of mind makes it even easier to involve personal feelings and experience in the discussion. If you can compare two characters' attitudes about an issue, adding your own view seems like a natural third perspective to include. The girls don't feel put on the spot to disclose, and the mothers, with a comfortable entry into the conversation, seem more able to relax and leave the lectures behind.

You may want to spend a few minutes during one of your early meetings talking about how to develop questions that fuel a lively discussion. Or just talk about it, and do it for fun, with your daughter during home reading time.

Got a Good Question? Act It Out!

Play-acting is a great way to bring issues to life for girls of any age.

Abstract thinking is a developmental step and it may be difficult sometimes to have a discussion about an abstract idea—like self-esteem or relationships—with younger girls. Before they're ten or eleven most girls take people and situations very literally, and if it makes sense in the story and makes sense in terms of what they know about people in their lives, then they don't have many questions. But you can ask the girls to play-act a character or act out one of the scenes in the book, or have the mothers play the scene and have some fun with the story.

You might go to a point in the story where you have a concern and say: "I thought that was a really strange part of the book" or "That part really bothered me, why don't we play it? Who wants to be the girl? Who wants to be the mother? Let's see if we can understand it or try different ways the scene could go."

The girls—as characters—can explore the situation in their own words and thoughts, and you can listen to their responses and learn a lot about what they know and don't know, and what they think. It gives girls a chance to bring their knowledge and questions in without having to make that kind of intellectual leap to the abstract issue. By role-playing a scene you approach the issue one step away from firm reality, but a step closer than the girls might experience it just by talking about it.

It allows you to ask questions without putting the girls on the spot. It gives everybody a real feeling of collaboration—and it's fun!

—ELIZABETH DEBOLD

A few other tips for developing good questions:

* Avoid questions that can be answered with a yes or no.

* When in doubt, ask "why?"

* Ask questions that pull you back to the text to find out how you "know" something. Is it because the author or a character said it right out, or have you assumed something? Could there be a different conclusion?

* Ask about motives. Why *did* a character do what she did? Or why would she?

* Ask about details. Why did the author make it storm that night—what did that allow to happen in the story? What did the character's clothing or choice of foods tell about him? Why would the author want us to know that?

* Why did characters feel the way they did? Are their feelings spelled out, or do you sense them in some other way? How?

* Explore language. Do the characters talk in a way that tells you something about them?

DISCUSSION:
HOW TO KEEP IT SIMMERING

Our discussions usually begin as the host daughter introduces the book, gives a short synopsis of the story and then presents her first question to get things started. Sometimes girls will raise their hands and wait for her to call on them; sometimes they just spontaneously toss out a thought or comment. The hosting daughter is the only girl who needs to have questions ready, so the other girls really are eager to hear them and start talking. Usually the discussion moves quickly, but everyone who wants a say gets it. And if the leader notices that someone hasn't said much, she may ask that person to pitch in a thought.

Early on the moms wondered if we'd need to establish some

THE ART OF DISCUSSION:
ADVICE FROM THE GIRLS

"If you talk about interesting things, then it keeps people wanting to talk. Ask questions like, 'Who was your favorite character,' or 'What part did you like the best?'"

—ASHLEY B.

"If you're the discussion leader, don't keep choosing the same people to answer questions all the time."

—BRITTNEY

"Sometime the moms will get a little carried away. The host will ask one question and the moms will get into this huge discussion. But then somebody—one of the girls—will just say, 'Can we get back to the discussion?'"

—MORGAN

"Moms should let girls answer the questions first, so the girls get a chance to talk."

—BRITTNEY

"One question that can be interesting is 'What would you do if you found yourself in this situation?'"

—MAYA

"The mothers should help make sure that everyone has a chance to answer questions and each person feels that she is an important part of the club."

—REBECCA

rules about interrupting and hand raising and the like, but we've discovered the same heartening thing over and over again. When the girls know they're in charge, they take charge quite effectively, working these things out in a most respectful and responsible way.

Once the mothers got used to the feeling of their daughters being in charge, we discovered how refreshing it was to sit back and enjoy the experience. We found that we listened more objectively, we reflected more calmly and we enjoyed being heard as equals within the group.

"In discussion, you want to open opportunities and don't want to foreclose on possibilities."

NINA BAYM

One way to help yourself step back from the coaching role and enhance the discussion and participation by the girls is to try what Bonnie Diamond, an elementary school language arts specialist, calls her "thirty-second rule." In her classroom discussions, when she poses a question, she pauses a full thirty seconds before calling on any student to answer. This gives everyone a few moments to collect her thoughts. It also slows the pace of the discussion—which otherwise can race at runaway speeds with young talkers—and makes it more inviting for the shy or reflective thinkers to join in.

A relaxed version of that works well for a mother-daughter discussion group, too. If the mothers simply try to refrain from prompting, or otherwise stepping in, for about thirty seconds, it gives the girls time to think. If a question hits a dead end with no response after that generous pause, then it may help for a mom to rephrase or reframe a question to help the discussion along. If discussion stalls out, put everyone at ease by acknowledging it and suggesting another line of thought. Real-life discussions aren't scripted like they are on TV. It's good for us all to feel the pace of genuine reflection and thoughtful conversation.

It may take a little practice to pause—we're all so accustomed to responding to everything and everyone as quickly as possible. But it's worth the try.

"Silence can be uncomfortable for people—even just a few

LESSONS FOR LIFE: PASSING THEM ON

Family stories can be a way of handing lessons down from one generation to the other. My grandmother used to tell us different kinds of stories. When she was trying to make a point about determination, she'd tell us one story. When she was trying to make a point about virtue, she'd tell others.

My great-grandmother was a teenage slave girl, and as such she was forbidden to have books or any reading material. Later, as a free woman she placed a great importance on education for her children. And she shared the stories of her life. Her daughter, my grandmother, used to tell us this story about her making the beds in the "big house." Because the beds were so high they used to use a long broomstick to reach across and push that bedspread under that pillow to make the fold.

One day, my great-grandmother was making the bed that way when the master's son came into the room and attempted to molest her. Well, she had been so conditioned to protect her virtue that she hit him with this stick! Her mistress complimented her for protecting her virtue, but then gave her a whipping for being so audacious or bold as to hit the master's son.

My grandmother told us the story in order to point out the importance of being virtuous and of not letting anyone talk you out of your virtue, no matter how important or powerful they might be. That experience, passed down in that story, has affected all of the girls and women in our family.

—BERTHA WATERS

Sharing Lives and Leaving Lectures Behind

Excerpt from *The Man in the Ceiling*

Jimmy nodded in the same way he did when Mother took
him forcibly by the hand to the Museum of Modern Art in
New York and made him look. Jimmy didn't mind art if he
could see it alone and decide for himself what he liked and
what he didn't. But when it came to art, his mother was
like his teachers. The questions she responded to were her
own, not Jimmy's. And the more she lectured him about
Picasso and Braque and Cézanne, the more the canvases
on the wall began to remind him of math problems on
Mrs. Minnafy's blackboard. . . .

"You don't have to lecture to 'speak from experience,'" says psychologist Elizabeth Debold. "For instance, if there's a girl in the story who
is overly concerned about her appearance or her weight, could that be
something that the girls or women have had to struggle with or are
familiar with in their own lives? To engage in a discussion, the women
present can ask themselves, 'Is there a place in my experience that I can
speak from?' Think about sharing experience rather than lecturing or
wanting to lecture about the perils of eating disorders or whatever."

—ELIZABETH DEBOLD

seconds of it," says Kathie. "But I like to wait it out and see where the girls take the discussion naturally, where it goes."

Don't feel questions have to be "hard" or complex to inspire good discussion. Simple questions have great discussion potential when they ask what the reader thinks or feels. Nina Baym shares her experience as a professor in the college classroom:

"I used *Little Women* as the basis for a discussion in a class of undergraduate women. I had assumed that Jo would be everybody's favorite character, but that wasn't the case," she says. "Some identified with Amy —she was ambitious and wanted to be an artist—and some identified with Meg. Nobody identified with Beth because she died, but what I assumed to be automatic wasn't the case at all. So you can ask: 'Who's the main character?' and you'd be surprised in some cases."

> ### BOOKS TO GROW ON
>
> These are books from my childhood that I still love to read:
>
> The Bible
>
> *Winnie the Pooh*
> A. A. Milne
>
> *The Secret Garden*
> Frances Hodgson Burnett
>
> *The Yearling*
> Marjorie Kinnan Rawlings
>
> *A Tale of Two Cities*
> Charles Dickens
>
> —MARY RODGERS, AUTHOR
> *Freaky Friday*

BOOKS AND AUTHORS:
LET THEM BE YOUR HELPERS

In group discussion, the books become your partners, your teachers, your tools. They give you the benefit of someone else's research, someone else's wisdom, to help you explore an issue. Whenever you get mothers and daughters talking, the daughters don't all the time hear the mothers, and mothers don't all the time hear them, but they can hear each other through the book— it bridges the communication gap. You can step out of yourself as an individual and into your role as part of a group, which gives you the ability to deal openly with issues that might be difficult one-on-one.

The comfort level of discussion within our circle lets us take some of these touchy questions home to talk about there. And sometimes it works the other way—bringing conversations from home to the club—as Alice recalls about our time with the book *Julie of the Wolves*:

"There's a part in *Julie* where the little girl has been promised in marriage to a little boy and at thirteen she goes to marry this little boy. One evening the little boy decides he needs to consummate the marriage. Nothing actually happens because the little girl runs away," Alice notes, "but I hadn't told Holly that this issue was in there. She came to me alarmed when she read it, and said, 'Is this sexual abuse? Is this right? Is this fair?' I had to stop and think: 'Now that I've introduced it, what do I do, where do I go with it?'

"We talked about the cultural aspects of it, how the marriage was an accepted part of that culture, and how it still goes on in some cultures," Alice says. "Of course, when it came up at book club discussion, Holly blurted out that it was sexual abuse. Some of the girls giggled. A lot of them didn't even want to discuss it. There was a shyness about it, but a sense that something was wrong about it. From that point on, when they needed to refer to that period of time in the story, they'd say 'that time.'"

We had been curious to see what the girls' perception of this situation was, and how we could help them to better understand it as a cultural issue. Unable to make much of an impression with talk of cultures, finally one of the mothers asked the girls if they would like their parents to arrange their marriage. There was a resounding "No!" Once we were speaking their language, they knew just how to speak their minds.

The discussions always hold more surprises for us—more discovery—when we aren't directing them. Sometimes we expect a discussion of some issue to take off because we're *ready* for it, and the girls skip right past us and down some other avenue of

BOOKS TO GROW ON

My daughter and I had (and still have) a very special relationship. I never had any sisters and therefore never experienced as a child the wonderful children's books Elizabeth and I explored together. Nothing can ever take those hours away from either of us. She still remembers our reading *Caddie Woodlawn* while she was sick with the flu in fourth grade. And every once in a while, when she's sick, we'll be talking and she'll say, "I wish you were here to read a little *Caddie Woodlawn* to me, Dad." Those are the lifetime relationships that are built with family reading.

Here's my list of favorites:

PICTURE BOOKS:

Madeline, Ludwig Bemelmans

Good Griselle, Jane Yolen

Monster Mama, Liz Rosenberg

NOVELS:

The Bears' House, Marilyn Sachs

Bella Arabella, Liza Fosburgh

A Blue-Eyed Daisy, Cynthia Rylant

The Day It Rained Forever, Virginia T. Gross

Caddie Woodlawn, Carol Ryrie Brink

The Girl with the Silver Eyes, Willo Davis Roberts

Roll of Thunder, Hear My Cry, Mildred D. Taylor

Words by Heart, Ouida Sebestyen

—JIM TRELEASE, AUTHOR
The Read-Aloud Handbook

thought. We may try to pursue the idea by asking a question or pulling their attention to it, and sometimes it brings about a good stretch of conversation. But you never know. The girls are just as likely to giggle, groan or otherwise shrug it off. That's when it's important to stop and listen and hear what they're telling us— they're not interested, maybe *not ready*, and the topic is best just left for the moment.

It's not forgotten, though. Inevitably the idea resurfaces during conversations at home, or for no apparent reason when we're reading the next book. The candor and comfort level that we enjoy with each other at our Mother-Daughter Book Club meetings carry over to the unlimited horizons of daily life. As it turns out, the Mother-Daughter Book Club discussions aren't an end point in the study of a book. They're a starting point in our mother-daughter relationships for exploring and sharing our lives.

ENDNOTES

✶ Encourage the girls to lead discussion—not the mothers.

✶ A good question is the key to a good discussion. When in doubt, ask "Why?"

✶ Let the book and the author guide your discussion. Act out scenes from books to spark conversation.

CHAPTER SEVEN

THE
MOTHER~DAUGHTER
DIALOGUE

It is the responsibility of every adult — especially parents,

educators and religious leaders — to make sure that children hear

what we have learned from the lessons of life, and to hear over and over

that we love them and that they are not alone.

—MARIAN WRIGHT EDELMAN

Founder and President, Children's Defense Fund

JAMEXIS & ALEXIS CHRISTIAN

Hello, my name is Jamexis and I'm twelve and in sixth grade at National Cathedral School. I like to play all different kinds of sports a lot, and I like sculpting and carving clay in art. I've played clarinet in the band at school for two years, too. And I like to go horseback riding. At home I like to play with my dog Snowball, a Maltese terrier. I also like to play games on the computer.

Animals are special to me. I understand them and love to read about them and sort of protect them when I see people doing something that isn't good for them. I'd like to be an artist and a veterinarian some-day. The most unusual thing I've ever done was, on a trip to Hawaii, I swam with dolphins! They feel like wet rubber and it was a little scary because you can see all their little teeth, but they don't bite.

I'm special in the way I look at things differently. Like, if someone shows me a picture of somebody running after a duck, I see it one step further and like to make up stories about why they were running or where they were going.

My mother is a health care representative and talks with doctors a lot. On weekends she likes to vacuum and clean the house. She also likes to listen to music and sew—she makes clothing and stuff—and she likes to sit there and read books.

I like to read where there's no one else around. I just get into reading the book and imagining what's happening. It's like I'm inside the book. My favorite books are *Homesick, The Man in the Ceiling* and *The House of Dies Drear*.

I really like to read reference books that illuminate the lifestyles of different animals—especially horses, dogs and cats. I learned that when dogs roll over, they're showing you they're submissive and you're the boss. I read these books because I plan to be a vet and want to get a head start on my education in this area.

The script for motherhood was written a long time ago. You'd think it would have improved over the centuries, but here we are, heading for the year 2000, and the dialogue still comes down to something like this:

MOTHER: Hurry up or you'll be late to class!

DAUGHTER: I can't find my shoes.

MOTHER: Where did you take them off?

DAUGHTER: They aren't there.

MOTHER: Nobody came along and took your shoes. Wherever you left them is where they are. If you put things where they belong, you can find them when you need them. The same thing goes for your homework, your clothes—I left your folded clothes on the bed a week ago and you haven't put them away yet—if you'd keep your room clean, you could find—

DAUGHTER: Mom, I found my shoes!

MOM: Where?

DAUGHTER: Where I left them. Hurry up, Mom, you're making me late for class!

It isn't the kind of dialogue that melts naturally into a thoughtful sharing of inner lives. In fact, from the sound of things around our house, it would be natural for my daughter to think my interests in life are laundry, meals, homework and getting places on time. That and forcing other people to think my way about laundry, meals, homework and getting places on time.

Maybe I'm a little oversensitive to patterns in history—it is, after all, something I work with a lot as a museum administrator. But from one busy day to the next, I hear the age-old pattern of mother-daughter dialogue playing out all around me.

As Morgan was turning nine, I could see that pattern of communication taking shape in our lives. There were days when most of our conversations—if you could call them that—fell into one of two categories: maintenance or compliance. I was on her case about everything. I didn't mean to be. I did it because I thought she needed the direction. She didn't see it that way at all, of course, and said so. We were both getting weary of the debate.

Other mothers were telling me similar stories about the mother-daughter dialogue in their own homes. We all had the same wistful conclusions: we could see adolescence looming for our daughters, and we wanted to strengthen our relationships with them while there was still time—before they became teenagers and completely lost interest in us.

I thought about how I only began to really get to know my own mother a few years ago when she came to live with us for a time after she suffered a stroke. One day during that time, I was astonished to hear her playing our piano. I had no idea she could play. Turns out she'd learned as a girl, and it had been a source of pleasure to her all these many years. How could I not know that? The truth was, we had a lot of unexplored territory between us, and that visit began our belated effort to step beyond our generational identities and get to know each other, one good woman to another.

When I thought about Morgan, and the kind of relationship I wanted to enjoy with her as the years press on, I knew I had to change the script somehow and I wanted to do it *now*.

The quality of our relationship was nobody's priority but mine, and the demands of housework, homework, after-school activities, and family, community and professional life weren't going to change. I knew that good intentions weren't enough; I'd had those for nine years.

When my thoughts turned to the idea of a mother-daughter book club, it felt promising. The experience of our first organizational meeting delivered on that promise of creating a space in our lives where we could talk about ideas, ourselves and each other. Our Mother-Daughter Book Club experience has, in fact, changed the script of mother-daughter relationships, for all of us, in more ways than we ever imagined—all of them good.

SHARING: A CIRCLE OF TRUST AND TRUTH

You can sit by yourself and enjoy a good book. But something very different and special happens when you get together and talk about a book with other people. You experience the book differently. Discussion becomes a prism, breaking the book's events, characters and themes into a rainbow of ideas that lead the way to still more discussion. Things we thought were obvious can become intriguing; the ordinary can become interesting. The assumptions that so often define our attitudes toward each other as mothers and daughters, and which limit our experience of each other, can fall away.

With their friends, the girls feel the strength and security to say things that, alone, they just wouldn't say to your face. They feel fortified. The respect for their mothers is still there, but the veil is lifted.

"We don't always see things from the same perspective, but we encourage them," Cheryl says. "There's a lot of respect between the mothers and daughters. Part of this is about helping them learn to think independently and not be overly influenced by another's opinion—even when the 'other' is your mother."

> *"When I look at my daughter, I can see that in many ways we're the same and in many ways we're different. My job, as a mother, is to help her become what she wants and needs to become, rather than what I may wish. Her dreams will become her life."*
>
> HARRIET MOSATCHE
> *Director of Program Development, Girl Scouts of the U.S.A.*

Sometimes the moments of discovery have nothing to do with the books at all, but the fact that we're all together just relaxed and talking about things, speaking what's on our minds.

For instance, one of our mothers mentioned to the group that she was facing a potential promotion at work with some mixed feelings because it would require that she work year round instead of the nine-month school year. "I hope you don't get it,"

AN AUTHOR'S FAMILY HISTORY: STRONG WOMEN AND STORYTELLING

In the first year of our Mother-Daughter Book Club, we read four books by Virginia Hamilton: *Cousins, Her Stories, The House of Dies Drear,* and *The Mystery of Drear House.* Mothers and daughters alike were swept into these powerful stories; the characters and events come up time and time again in our discussions of new selections and life themes. In this interview, Ms. Hamilton shares with us a bit of *her story*:

"I came from a storytelling family. My parents were great story-tellers—my mother particularly. My mother *told stories*. It's something she did all the time. The first one I ever heard was of my grandfather's escape from slavery to this part of Ohio. So often the subtexts of my stories are from that period of time and that place.

"One of the books that particularly impressed me when I was younger was by Shirley Graham, who became the wife of black scholar W. E. B. Du Bois. She wrote a book called *There Was Once a Slave*—the biography of Frederick Douglass—and for me it made him come to life. I read that and said, 'I'd like to do that.'

"Storytelling was the way my family passed along cultural learn-ing—the family's lineage, for instance. My family had been in Ohio for six or seven generations, so it gave you a sense of history because everyone talked and nobody told the story the same way twice. It was a wonderful way of being together, talking and spending time together.

"My father was a classical mandolinist and traveled widely, setting up these mandolin clubs all over the country. He met my mother in Canada—she said that when she met him she knew that was the man for her, and they were married some time later. She told stories about it all. My father told me about the last great camps of the High Plains Indians because he saw all that. I came by dialogue at an early age, knowing that talking had a beginning, a middle and an ending. As soon as I could write, I could write dialogue.

"My mom and dad let us grow and learn. There were only three things I had to do: Be home before dark. I had to be on the honor roll. And I had to not play too hard—I used to get nightmares if I did that. That was about all. We had a twelve-acre farm. My uncles all had farms, and you could play all day and never leave family land. It was a very secure place; the outside world didn't often get into ours.

"My mother was very strong; all the women in my family were. She had her circle. The women were very vital in my life. I write my books for everyone to read—*girls and boys*—but I do write books that are often female-oriented. In my books, the female characters are always searching for something and they often find it, and what they find is themselves and their own strength. I want girls to understand there has been a long history of strong women and women doing their own kinds of work for a very long time. Women have always been oppressed but managed to see their own way, and there is a long tradition of females doing what they want to do, and that's what *girls* can do. They can have selves of their own, a definition of themselves.

"Me? What I do is write and I really enjoy it. That's what I do. That's the important thing."

her daughter declared. "I like the time we get to spend together in the summers." She hadn't told her mother how she felt about the situation before, but the comfort level in our circle made it easier for her to say something difficult. It gave them a bridge for talking more about it later, just the two of them.

There's a certain level of trust built into the group, too. We're here as pairs of mothers and daughters, but the understanding is that we're all individuals and this is a place where we speak for ourselves and listen respectfully to each other. We don't interrupt or correct the girls as they speak. We don't try to make over their answers to please ourselves or to fit an image we wish they would project. And we don't feel responsible for what our "partner" says. We're all there to explore. We really don't know what the girls are going to say about some subjects as they arise. At times the things they say may make us squirm a little, but the feeling is: we're among friends.

Here's a snippet of the discussion that arose one day when talk turned from the characters in the book to the characters at home:

MOTHER: This is maybe a dangerous question: Do your moms get depressed?

GIRL: Yes. (*laughter*)

MOTHER: Do you all do anything to help us when we're depressed? What do you do?

GIRL: I try to get my momma to come back.

GIRL: When she goes in the library, I talk with Daddy.

GIRL: I usually try to leave my mom alone because she just gets stressed.

One afternoon's discussion took an unexpected turn when the girls picked up on a scene in the book in which the character retreats to the bathroom when she wants to be alone. Her family's apartment is so cramped and crowded that she has nowhere else to go. One mom asked the girls if they had a special place at home where they went when they wanted to be alone. Instead of answering the question, one daughter mentioned that when her mom and dad have an argument her mom goes to the study to be alone.

From there, we moved back to the book to answer the next question, and the discussion forged ahead to new material.

When I play that scene back in my mind, I see points at which we could have squelched the discussion with a motherly quip—"Let's talk about something else." We could have sweetly shamed them into dropping the topic by saying something like "Let's move on—we don't want to embarrass anybody."

Believe me, it was tempting. But we kept to our good intentions and they worked! The girls were able to share their experiences, we learned more about how they see things and we were able to contribute a few thoughts before they turned back to reflect on their own feelings and the universal need, at times, for a place to be alone with one's thoughts.

I couldn't have planned it better myself.

BOOKS TO GROW ON

Here is a booklist my sixteen-year-old twin daughters (Mavis Gruver and Nia Kelly) and I came up with:

Moon Over Crete,
Jyotsna Sreenivasan

A Wrinkle in Time,
Madeleine L'Engle

Pride and Prejudice,
Jane Austen

The Secret Garden,
Frances Hodgson Burnett

To Kill a Mockingbird,
Harper Lee

Up the Down Staircase,
Bel Kaufman

An Outbreak of Peace,
Sarah Pirtle

Finding My Voice,
Marie G. Lee

Women Who Run with the Wolves,
Clarissa Pinkola Estes

Sula,
Toni Morrison

Twelfth Night,
William Shakespeare

New Moon: The Magazine for Girls and Their Dreams

—NANCY GRUVER, PUBLISHER
New Moon magazine

READING BOOKS, SHARING STORIES, SHARING LIVES

I am a daughter, too, after all. I was young once. Think about who you were at age nine or ten, and where you were in your thinking and your understanding of the world. When I think about life as I knew it at ten, I'm not sure what's memory—memory of real things—and what's images of stories I heard over and over as a child. Even more than the facts, I recall impressions I had of the people and events going on around me. I remember feelings—feelings of comfort, delight, pride or disappointment. The fact is, all of it counts; all of it shapes the life of a girl.

Clearly, no matter what we say, as mothers, our daughters hear us through their own experience. And they "hear" that mother-daughter dialogue through our actions even more than our words.

I can tell Morgan that I respect her intelligence, that I like to hear what she thinks about things and that I want our relationship to include a feeling of friendship as we both grow older. The words tell her what I think, but our Mother-Daughter Book Club discussions give me a place to show her what I mean.

We've also noticed that the girls respond differently to our comments when we make them at group. We all respond differently, in fact. When someone expresses disagreement over a point, it's taken as a springboard for more talk—not a personal complaint that has to be remedied. When a mother shares a life story or view, it isn't told or heard as a lecture, as it so often seems to be at home. The girls listen. Sometimes they'll pick the thought up for discussion. Other times, they want to move on.

"In discussion, you hear it from your point of view and your mom's point of view, and sometimes they're different and sometimes they're the same," Jihan says. "It's definitely more interesting."

Jamexis adds: "When the mothers start talking, it's different than when the children are talking. The mothers talk deeply about things, with different insights."

An observation from Holly offers a slightly different perspective on the same scene: "One thing I've found out is girls really like to read, and mothers can really talk," Holly says. "We answer questions and it's in like five sentences at the most. The moms talk in paragraphs."

These old moms' tales don't go totally unappreciated, however. Says Brittney: "It's okay when the mothers talk about things. You can learn about what happened to other people when they were little."

And Ashley B. offers this definitive piece of sage advice: "I would tell moms not to go on and on about what happens to them. That just makes the discussion longer and boring. We like hearing their stories some, but if they think it's going to be a long, boring one they shouldn't start it. If it's short and interesting, that's okay."

Okay. So we do sometimes get a little carried away with expressing our views. But we never gang up on the girls with motherly advice. In fact, the mothers often have different perspectives on a discussion point. But the presence of several mothers in the discussion seems to lend some credibility to each mother when she makes a point of her own.

"It's been very good to talk to other moms with girls the same age," Grace says. "It shows you that what you're going through—the developmental stuff—you're not going through alone. You learn how others have dealt with these issues. We can talk about issues that otherwise we wouldn't take the time to do. We've developed wonderful relationships with the moms."

Our reading selections, and our group discussions, give all of us—girls and women alike—a feeling of shared lives. Sometimes we find company in the characters or authors we meet through our books. I'm not the only woman struggling to balance responsibilities and desires in my life, as well as in the lives of those I love. Sometimes we find support or encouragement as we compare our lives or thoughts with those we're reading, or share our own tales from the front. Whose fact, whose fiction? It doesn't matter. We're all on the same field trip, taking in some views. It's all part of the landscape.

MOTHERS AND DAUGHTERS
IN THE CLASSICS

Seeing the mothers and daughters in classic literature interact is so enlightening because the girls all related to their mothers in very different ways than children relate to their mothers today. And mothers interacted with their children quite differently.

The thing that fascinated me most was I found there are so many wonderful parenting techniques modeled—wonderful things to do with children and how to talk with children, even how to effectively discipline or motivate them to do certain things. In *Little Women, Anne of Green Gables* and the Little House books, all these girls interact with their mothers or a mother figure in very real ways.

All the mothers—and including the mother figure in *Anne of Green Gables*—were very sensitive, but they were strict and had a definite plan as to how their children should behave, how they should develop as people, about their moral development. And it wasn't preachy. In *Little House*, when Laura was about to do something a little naughty, all Ma had to do was say, "Laura," and Laura knew she had better shape up. The mothers had very definite expectations about behavior and yet they weren't unreasonable.

What this did was it gave children a measure of confidence that they could connect with the adult world, they could be in the adult world, and yet be accepted as children.

—CAROLYN STROM COLLINS, AUTHOR
The World of Little House, The Anne of Green Gables Treasury, The Little Women Treasury

LEARNING HOW TO LISTEN TO GIRLS

How is it that a child can get high marks for "listening skills" on a school report card and seem so totally oblivious to the spoken word at home? Am I the only mother who has to repeat requests for children to clean up rooms, put the milk in the refrigerator or get started on homework?

Listening means different things in different places. On a nature walk, it means to silence yourself and pay attention to the sounds around you. At school and at home it usually means to follow directions. Sometimes it means to learn a fact or a concept. Listening is something you almost always hear adults asking children to do. You just don't often hear children ask adults to listen, but that doesn't mean we shouldn't try it more often.

You might think of listening as a passive thing to do, but in our Mother-Daughter Book Club discussions, we put our listening skills through a real workout. We listen for opportunities to recognize every girl's contribution as important to the group, to encourage the quiet one to speak and the rushing one to reflect. We listen for the sound of their lives: for hints of courage or confidence that we can bolster, for misinformation or confusion we can clarify. As the discussion moves along, our girls are expressing themselves about issues and in ways that we may not often see at home, so the payoff for listening is that we learn more about them.

For all of us, but especially for the girls, the experience of being *listened to* is exciting.

They show obvious pride in leading discussion when it is their hosting day. And they've become more intent upon listening to others' comments and weaving the thoughts into the ongoing discussion. Being *listened to*, they have become better *listeners*.

We've discovered some pleasant side effects at home, too. Morgan, for instance, credits the Mother-Daughter Book Club with all manner of improvements in my attitude. In the past, we argued about her choices of clothes. Lately she likes my suggestions about clothes, explaining that "now that you know me better

MOTHERS AND DAUGHTERS: CELEBRATING OUR INDIVIDUALITY

We look at our daughters and we think: "They're our daughters and we should have this immediate connection and bond." Yet, that's not always the case. We have to listen and listen to them, and to ourselves.

We all carry our childhood selves with us. As mothers, we think we can empathize relatively easily with what it's like to be nine or thirteen or seventeen, but what we're remembering is what it was like *for us* to be nine or thirteen or seventeen, and the social context isn't the same.

Times change and people are different. People are individuals, and our daughters are individuals. We need to make sure we value our own individual selves. Then we can value our daughters' individuality, and not expect to relive our lives through our daughters—thinking of things we didn't do quite right and trying to make sure they "do it right." A lot of the difficulty comes from that: seeing them in terms of what we hope they might be, rather than seeing them for themselves.

I'm not sure we need to see things through their eyes. Rather, we need to understand they have their eyes and we have ours, and not expect them to see things as we do or us to see things as they do—we mothers have a much longer and different experience. They don't have the experience to know what we know, or even to know that we know it. We can't expect them to know. We didn't used to know it either.

It's better for all of us if our daughters can understand that we see things a little differently. Then there's a basis for dialogue. It's always illu-minating to be in any discussion of what our daughters read because it gets to what they think and like, and getting daughters to talk about what they like and read is the important thing.

Whether it's mothers and mothers, or mothers and daughters, or daughters and daughters, the more the opportunity we have to have those discussions, the more we learn about other people and ourselves.

—SUSAN MCGEE BAILEY
Executive Director, Wellesley Centers for Women

you pick out things I like." I honestly don't know whether I'm picking clothes differently, or if Morgan is simply more open to my suggestions. It doesn't matter. We've also noticed a definite drop in the decibel levels around the house—Morgan and I are communicating in quieter, calmer ways. We even complain more considerately.

Whatever it is, something has changed and we like it.

MOTHERS: SHARING
OUR WISDOM AND WONDER

I was at a long, sort of lonely business dinner one evening and during the cocktail hour I noticed a copy of the Smithsonian's Engagement Calendar, "Black Women Achieving Against the Odds," on a table. I hadn't seen it before, and as I glanced through it I came to a page entitled "Women in Politics." And there, in this panel of pictures, was a picture I remembered from a wall in my *grandmother's* house. *It was my great-aunt: Charlotta Spears Bass.* She was in the Smithsonian's book because she ran for vice president of the United States on the Progressive Party ticket in 1952. My vague memory was that it was some sort of family joke. *But it was true.* She had lived in California and had been the editor of the *California Eagle* newspaper. I remembered this tall, stately woman, my great-aunt coming from California; I saw her about twice in my life.

I think about her, and about my own mother, about the women whose pictures you see in other historic photographs, and the women whose lives and life's work have gone unrecognized—even in their own homes at times—and I feel that I'm here on the backs of so many women's shoulders, so many who have come before. We all are. If we want our girls to benefit from the courage and wisdom of the women before them, we have to share the stories.

I want Morgan to know who her mother is: that I'm human and I go through trials and tribulations. I want her to know that I struggle to satisfy my twin desires to nurture a strong, loving family and at the same time help make a strong, caring community through my professional work and volunteer efforts. I want her to have the sense that it's important not only to develop your talents for your own health and happiness, but also to give back to your community and help bring somebody else along.

There are things you'll see in reading a book together that you don't come across every day with your daughter, and this is your opportunity to explore those things. You can say, "Oh, I've been there," or "I've done that," or "I've wondered about that," or "I've felt that way." "What do you think about it? How do you feel?"

That is the most exciting part of the Mother-Daughter Book Club. The group discussions become a unique combination of intellectual and personal sharing. That's what brings mothers and daughters closer, and that's what gives all of us a special appreciation of each other as individuals.

COMPARING LIVES: MOTHERS, DAUGHTERS, FACT AND FICTION

None of us ever planned this as a continuing lecture in women's studies. For the mothers, that sounds too much like work. For the daughters, it sounds too much like school. But the girls enjoy the comparison aspect of discussion, so we use comparison as a framework for discussing the way girls and women are portrayed in our books and in life.

We look at the mother-daughter relationships in the stories—how authors portray them, or how a relationship contributes to a story. We look at how the culture of the time and place treats them, and how girls and women treat one another in the stories. Of course, we share our own experiences when it feels right.

Sometimes we're startled to hear what the girls think about the mother characters in a particular book. In the following discussion, the girls were comparing some mother figures, most of whom they had identified as "wimps" in one way or another. Then they picked out the mother in *The Man in the Ceiling* to give some pretty harsh judgment. Most of us mothers saw her as an intelligent woman, a caring mother and an artist trying to balance the demands and desires of work and family. Here's how it unfolded:

MOM: I don't understand what you mean when you say they're "wimpy." I take a little offense to it. And I'd like to have, at some point, some more discussion about that. The mothers make a difference in the lives of these children. And everyone's oblivious to the way these parents in the book function. They aren't loud and they aren't going out to the meetings and they aren't going to exciting things, but they make those families work.

GIRL: But they don't really do that much.

GIRL: In *The Man in the Ceiling*, the mom didn't do anything. She was very forgetful. She just went upstairs most of the time and would sit in that little room and paint.

MOM: She worked at home. She was an artist who worked out of her home.

GIRL: But she really didn't listen to anybody and nobody could bother her when she was up there.

MOM: Do you think that her children would be the people they are but for that mother? She provided an enormous amount of support.... .

GIRL: But she was also very forgetful.

MOM: But—it wasn't that you couldn't come, that she was trying to keep people out. She was making a clear separation between when she was working and when she was doing things in the house. So she was saying you couldn't just come up into her special place —disrespect the fact that she was working—come into her studio at just any time.

GIRL: But also, what if they needed something? Their dad usually wasn't there. He overworked.

MOM: That makes you think. When they thought they needed to

interrupt her, did they really need her? Was it really an emergency? Or were they just taking advantage of the fact that she's in the house?

MOM: Do you think that the father's work was more important than the mother's work?

GIRL: Before…it didn't say anything about the mother working ever.

MOM: You just told me she went to her room and she painted.

GIRL: Yeah, but it didn't say anything about the mother ever *selling* her picture.

MOM: So the only value is if she actually made money as an artist.

GIRL: Noooo, not necessarily. But if the dad was overworked, why couldn't she make a little bit of money, too?

MOM: Well, I am not a "working" mother and I love it. I would not trade this for anything in the world. And in fact, because I'm not working right now, with kids at this age, I'm able to do more of the kinds of things I think they need. But they don't seem to appreciate that… .

The discussion went on to touch on the roles mothers play in the books we read, and the roles they play in real life. Our group includes mothers who balance demanding professional careers and family, those who have stepped back from their successful professional careers to devote more time to family and those who devote full-time attention to family and community. The diversity of our roles, and our attitudes, adds to the depth of possibilities our girls see for motherhood, careers and individual pursuits.

The result is that without making this the "purpose" of the club or discussion, and without putting it on a written agenda, we explore the lives of girls and women. We identify the influences of history, culture and family on the lives we read about and the lives we live. We examine characters in full to discover the ways in which challenges strengthen or defeat them, and how individual courage or fear comes into play. It may be hard to imagine that such weighty topics could be fun, but the group makes it so.

MOTHERS: LEARNING FROM DAUGHTERS

The more we see of mothers and daughters in literature, the more we find to talk about and the closer to home the discussion drifts. Eventually the conversation and reflection settle on our own lives, and our own relationships as mothers and daughters. When we lay down the books and speak candidly about our own lives, our own stories, the characters glisten like teardrops; the plots unfold, surprising in some ways and shamelessly predictable in others. We are girls growing up—still—even as we speak. We are the mothers of whom our daughters speak. How can we fail to see the themes played out in these lives of ours?

"I was the brainy kid on the sideline," Leslye says. "My father was a chemist and my mother was a teacher and a guidance counselor—education and doing well in school were always stressed in my home because my parents believed that was the key to opportunities for blacks in the United States. I felt that pressure to be perfect and was the first black valedictorian in my high school. I had a few good friends, but most of my classmates probably viewed me as a Miss Goody Two Shoes, and I *was* different. I don't have fond memories of high school. It was nothing bad, but it wasn't an enjoyable time.

"Sometimes, when Brittney is having trouble finding close friends at school," Leslye says, "it's hard for me to know whether it's just normal for her age, or am I seeing too much of myself? We talk about it in terms of how it feels—that's something we both know and we can share our feelings."

When Linda's daughter Rebecca introduced her at our first club meeting, and someone asked what Linda "did," Rebecca made the now infamous remark—infamous in our circle, anyway—that "she lives." The fact was, Rebecca really didn't know what her mother did anymore since Linda had stepped off the fast

BOOKS TO GROW ON

These are books I've shared with children in urban neighborhoods whom I've known as a teacher or a friend. All of these, although in diverse ways, strike me as spiritual or religious books. Even Pooh has his transcendent days....

The House at Pooh Corner, A. A. Milne

Selected Poems, Gwendolyn Brooks

Night, Elie Wiesel

St. Francis of Assisi, Johannes Jergensen

Selected Poems, W. H. Auden

All Creatures Great and Small, James Herriot

Selected Poems of Langston Hughes, Langston Hughes

The Long Loneliness, Dorothy Day

—JONATHAN KOZOL, AUTHOR
Amazing Grace: The Lives of Children and the Conscience of a Nation

track on Capitol Hill to devote more time to her family at home. After some initial consternation, Linda reflected more thoughtfully on her daughter's words: "Rebecca has taught me a lot about life—what's important and what's not—and about living—focusing on what's important," Linda says now. "Before the Mother-Daughter Book Club, Rebecca never knew that I learn from her as much as she learns from me. I guess she had just never taken the time to think about it. It sort of hadn't occurred to me either."

Grace had been out of town on high-pressure work for days when she caught a flight that landed her at home in time to tuck her daughter Ashley into bed with some book club reading.

"It was two days before Ashley was supposed to go on this camping trip with some others," Grace says, "and she was packed and everything, and during our reading time that night she said, 'Mom—you know that camping trip? I want to talk with you about it, but I don't want you to be upset about it.' Then she told me she hates camping, she doesn't want to go, and hopes I won't get angry. We talked a lot about my past experiences camping, and hers, and finally I said, 'It's up to you.' You know, I don't think we ever would have had that talk if it hadn't been for our reading time and the fact that we've grown more comfortable talking about our feelings. That's what I want out of it. She'll grow up saying, 'My mom and I were in this book club....'"

Sometimes it is a simple theme of love and caring that we enjoy and want to perpetuate in our daughters' lives. Says Winnie: "The journey from childhood to adulthood to motherhood is an ongoing learning experience that recycles from generation to generation. Right now, I'm enjoying my second childhood through experiences with Tiffany. We love to travel together. And we discuss lots of things together. Tiffany is kind and gentle. I like being a mother; I like children. I wish I had a house full of children so we could sit in a circle at night, share our day and read books."

Even in lives where there is time enough for special moments, the Mother-Daughter Book Club remains a time-out of the nicest kind.

"We cook, we read, we do a lot together, but the club gives us a special place where Holly and I can be equals," Alice says. "As equals, we go to a book we haven't read before, and we analyze the book as equals. There are no right or wrong answers at the meeting and discussion, nobody's there to perform; just to share what we've gotten out of the book."

THE DAUGHTERS: LIVING AND LEARNING

The gap we feared would widen between our daughters and ourselves doesn't loom as large or as threatening in our thoughts anymore. As girls once, and mothers now, we know the distance will impose itself during the teen years ahead; it's only natural. But we know, as well, that the bridge of sharing we have established through our Mother-Daughter Book Club can span those years and beyond. The bridge is strong from both sides. The girls' views of us as individuals and their expressions of our role in their lives tell us that love can bridge the gap if you give it a way to get across.

Their comments make sweet background music for our literary and motherly endeavors:

"I can talk to my mom about anything and I like talking to her, says Ashley B. "She's smart. She has a sense of humor and I think she's a little playful. My mom is a really good friend. I love my mom very much."

"My mom encourages me," says Maya. "She helps me with my schoolwork but doesn't do it for me. Sometimes we disagree about clothes. She picks out dresses I don't really like or shoes I don't like. What I like best about her is she helps me, she likes my ideas and stuff like that. She loves me."

"My mom and I can talk to each other a lot more now," says Ashley S. "Like if there's something going on in school that's bothering me, I can talk about it with her and not worry."

"My mother is a kind of happy person—she likes to interact

MOTHERS' WISDOM:
REACHING OUT FOR PEACE

I was influenced by my mother's philosophy. She grew up in the apartheid of the South and the opportunities were nothing like we have now. Even so, my mom often said that hatred serves no purpose. I may be angry or mad about what happened, but you know, everyone who participated in this is dead now. We can be angry and sad about these things, but we need to have a chance to talk about them without going into corners and hating. You have to find a place for forgiveness.

If you're a mother, then the focus should be on your child, and if you focus on loving and caring and protecting that child, how much time do you really have to rail at the world? If you obsess about what's wrong in the world, you can spend your entire life focused on the stuff that's wrong. Fighting every day just wears you down, burns you out.

—CONNIE PORTER, AUTHOR
The American Girls Collection, Addy series

with other people" says Jamexis. "I've learned from her that you should always approach a person with an open mind and not judge them by what other people say about them. Think for yourself."

"My mom knows about me—somehow she knows what I'm going to do before I do it," Morgan told a friend who asked if the book club *really* made things better between us. "Some things we do the same—like save things and collect stuff. But we have different ideas about some other things. Like clothes. And now that she's getting to know me better, she's picking out clothes better, too."

MOTHERS & DAUGHTERS: MOVING AHEAD TOGETHER

I can't remember any other place or time in my life when I experienced this kind of talk among mothers and daughters. Every month our Mother-Daughter Book Club meets, we share more of literature and our lives, and it continues at home.

We're still grappling with laundry, meals, homework and getting places on time. But in larger, more meaningful ways, the mother-daughter dialogue is getting broader and better. The script is changing and it doesn't stop here.

MOTHERS AND DAUGHTERS:
TALKING FROM THE HEART

The essence of a close relationship between mother and daughter is truthfulness, a capacity to be able to talk about the whole range of our experience and to be able to understand that—to put into context the kinds of forces and pressures that affect both of us.

I know of a mother and a daughter who went shopping to buy the girl a formal dress for a dance. The daughter was kind of chunky, and none of the gowns looked right because she was bigger than the kind of body the designers had in mind when they designed these dresses. The mother and daughter began getting very upset, both of them, and then they began to get upset at each other.

The mother finally pulled herself up short and said: "You know, I'm getting really, really angry and I'm really angry that they make clothes only for anorexic girls." She stopped herself before getting furious at her daughter for being overweight and when she realized that—wait a minute—her daughter was not really overweight, her build was different, and this was a whole cultural, society thing that is done to women about our looks and weight.

When she put it that way, her daughter said, "Yeah, that makes me really mad and makes me feel bad." They began to have a conversation that was really different—the girl wasn't the problem, at all—and one that allowed them to stay connected.

Part of what is important about staying connected is being able to understand there are a lot of forces and pressures in our culture that are easy to get caught up in and not recognize. When we have some understanding of how that works, we can share a different and deeper kind of truthfulness between mother and daughter, a truthfulness that takes the blame away, allows us to keep perspective and be able to speak about these things.

—ELIZABETH DEBOLD

ENDNOTES

* The Mother-Daughter Book Club expands the range of mother-daughter dialogue.

* Girls speak (and listen) freely in the club setting—even when the conversation is not about books.

* Club discussions provide a springboard for mothers and daughters to talk more about an issue later, one-on-one.

* Mothers have as much to learn from their daughters as their daughters do from them—once they learn to listen.

CHAPTER EIGHT

GIRLS WILL BE GIRLS: AGE AND ATTITUDES

To everything there is a season,

and a time to every purpose under heaven.

—ECCLESIASTES

MAYA & JOYCE YETTE

My name is Maya Yette. I'm nine and I'm in fourth grade.

I like swimming and gymnastics. I also play the clarinet and the piano. At school I'm a safety patrol and I sing in the chorus. My favorite thing is the school newspaper. I'm an editor, but I also write stories—one of them was on display at the '96 Summer Olympics in Atlanta!

I want to be a veterinarian because I like animals. I have a rabbit and a canary. My canary is a female (males are TOO loud) and she lives in my room. When I first got her I kept a journal about her because I wanted to note her behavior.

When friends come over, we play with my pets. Sometimes we play Barbies or ride bikes or play outside in my tree house. Sometimes we play basketball. I'm on a basketball team and my dad, Fred, is the coach. I play different things with different friends, but everybody likes playing hide-and-seek in the dark.

I like reading a lot. My favorite books are mysteries and books about animals. I've read most of the Baby-sitter's Club books. My favorite characters are Dawn and Jessie—Dawn cares about animals and the environment, and Jessie is friendly and energetic. Me? I'm friendly and kind of quiet and sensitive. I think about things a lot. My mom says that's why I'm a good writer.

My mom's name is Joyce. She graduated from Harvard and is a lawyer. I like hearing her stories about growing up in South Carolina. My mom started making porcelain dolls when I was born. She collects dolls, too. She wanted to have a hobby that she could share with me and my sister Laila, who's six. Mom has a big collection of Madame Alexander dolls. She also helps me with my collections—seashells, keychains, paperdolls and "God's Eyes," the designs you make with yarn and popsicle sticks. I wish my mom knew how to sew, then she could teach me. Then we could make doll clothes instead of buying them.

The best thing about my mom is that she takes care of me and loves me, and listens to me and likes my ideas.

A couple times a year, when the clutter in Morgan's room grows so thick and looms so large that I can no longer overlook it, I stage an ambush. She's never there, of course. She couldn't imagine parting with the cardboard backing pieces from packages of decorative stickers, or the scraps of notes or the valentine cards from last year's school party. I can.

I'm often moved to action around her birthday in the fall, and again at the end of the school year. I think perhaps both calendar moments carry a special sense of time passing, of Morgan growing, and reasonably *outgrowing*, some of the trappings of the year past. As I sift through the layers of clutter, tossing into a trash bag that which is rightly trash and trying to decide which other things to pass on to Morgan's younger sister, I am reminded that a child's age alone is not always a useful measure. It's not Morgan's *age* I'm thinking of as I search for the toys and things she has "outgrown" and can pass on to others. It's *Morgan*: her likes and dislikes, her interests, skills and talents, her emotional maturity and life experience.

> *"She's ten now, so she doesn't talk as much to me anymore. The Mother-Daughter Book Club has been great for helping to keep the communication going. It gives us a special time together. And it gives us a lot to talk about."*
>
> LINDA CHASTANG

Certainly, age is a consideration as we select books for our Mother-Daughter Book Club, and in our expectations about discussion and socializing. It played a role at the organizational stage of our club, too. We aimed for girlfriends basically the same age or grade level. But the exception—the friend who was a full year younger and grade lower than the others—has been no more giggly than her older friends, and no less insightful in her contributions to discussion. Rather than focus strictly on a girl's age as you organize your group, or scout books for them to read, it may be more useful to think about a girl's interests, maturity, her reading skills and confidence level in group discussion. If a book, or club, provides a comfort zone for a girl in each of those areas, then it's likely to be a good fit.

MAKING AGE-APPROPRIATE SELECTIONS: THE PLOT THICKENS

The mothers were ready. Our secret agendas were in place: In the book *Cousins,* that annoyingly perfect and reed-thin Patty Ann character had a problem she thought no one knew about: an eating disorder. Secretly, she would make herself throw up after meals. It was mentioned only in passing, in a scene where her teenage cousin—belittled, angry and looking for some way to shatter that flawless composure—taunts her about "upchucking" and idly threatens to tell her mother. The issue presents itself and is gone in a less than a page; the story moves on.

In the reality of life for adolescent girls these days, eating disorders are no idle threat. They are among the many self-destructive responses experts say are growing more common among girls and women who are struggling with issues of self-image, self-esteem and lack of power in their lives. Among the mothers in our group, the feeling was unanimous: *Here* was something that needed *talking* about. When does the conversation at home just naturally turn to eating disorders? This was our moment.

So when the discussion began with a comparison of girl characters from different books the group had read, one mother asked if all of these characters were happy. Here's the dialogue that unfolded among the moms and girls:

GIRL: Yeah, they had good grades and everything else.

MOM: Were they happy?

GIRL: No. Well, Patty Ann was happy.

BOOKS TO GROW ON

Sophie's World,
Jostein Gaarder

Go Tell It on the Mountain,
James Baldwin

Another Country,
James Baldwin

Selected Poems of Emily Dickinson
Emily Dickinson

Raisin in the Sun,
Lorraine Hansbury

The Bluest Eye,
Toni Morrison

—RITA DOVE

SENSITIVE SUBJECTS:
WHEN MOTHERS CARE ENOUGH TO TALK

There are difficult issues you need to talk about. But who wants to talk about race and sex discrimination? Look at the book *Amazing Grace*, by Mary Hoffman. I really love the way she writes about both of those issues and does it with such sensitivity.

The story is about a little girl who wants to be Peter Pan in the school play. There are kids who say she can't possibly do it because Peter Pan wasn't black, and she is. And because Peter Pan wasn't a girl. But there is a grandmother figure in the story, and she tells Grace, "You can be anything you want, if you put your mind to it." There are so many aspects of the book that I appreciate: There is the figure of the grand-mother, and the idea of the extended family. My mother is seventy-three years old, and every time she comes to my house she wants to read *Amazing Grace.*

People will ask me, about the Addy books, "Why do you want to write about slavery? There's so much else to write about."

I can understand their concern. But this is our history and if we sidestep it, it's because we're uncomfortable and not because our chil-dren are uncomfortable. These are our great-great-grandfathers and grandmothers I'm writing about. Their voices need to be heard, and nobody heard them for so very long and very few people cared about what they thought. I feel I've been blessed to talk about someone's life.

—CONNIE PORTER

GIRL: No...

MOM: You think Patty Ann was happy?

GIRL: Well, she wasn't happy because she didn't have a lot of friends, but she was happy because she was pretty and because she got good grades.

GIRL: I say no, she wasn't.

MOM: What about—why did she make herself throw up?

GIRL: Because she thought she was fat.

GIRL: And she also didn't like her food....

MOM: She thought she was pretty, and she was always very good at things and she knew that. She believed she was better than the others....

GIRL: But she wasn't really happy, because she got good grades so that her mother wouldn't get mad at her—

GIRL: Yeah, but she had some happiness, like playing the piano and rehearsing.

GIRL: That's true.

MOM: Was it her decision to take piano, to rehearse?

GIRL: I think it was her decision to play piano and practice some.

MOM: Did anyone feel differently? Did anyone think it was someone else's decision?

MOM: How many people take piano? How many people love to practice?

MOM: I think Patty Ann took real pleasure in her talents.

MOM: I think Patty Ann was thrilled to be the best that she could be. Some of the things, certainly, she was pushed into being, but I think she was happy also.

MOM: My sense is that she was very unhappy. When young ladies have eating disorders it usually suggests they are unhappy. Maybe not about something specific, but they're generally not happy people. It's something that's eating at them from the inside that shows up as an eating disorder.

GIRL: They think they're fat.

MOM: Then appearance is very important to them....

MOM: And an eating disorder is also a manifestation of her not having any control of anything else but what goes in her and so she is getting rid of that. That is the only thing she has control of. Her mom is controlling everything else.

MOM: I really am curious about why the mothers are so divided about whether she was happy or not. What do you girls feel?

GIRL: I know she's happy at some things that she chooses. But she's unhappy to think she's going to be fat.

GIRL: I think she's half and half.

GIRL: I think she's happy about her hair and her piano and everything.

The discussion went on to explore how different characters showed they were happy or unhappy.

MOM: When I read the book at first I thought that Patty Ann was happy wearing beautiful clothes, having very long hair, being adored—she loved being adored. And the reason she had the eating disorder and the reason she was mean to some people, was that she was afraid that people wouldn't like her if she changed. She was afraid if she gained weight people wouldn't like her. She was afraid that if she didn't have pretty clothes people wouldn't like her. So, now, after thinking about it, I come out thinking that Patty Ann was really kind of sad.

MOM: Happiness is really generated from feeling good about yourself, and having friends and a supportive family. She thought she had to have long hair and play the piano and get straight A's to get that. But what she really wanted was the love and warmth you get from friends and family.

MOM: I tend to disagree with that because I don't think you should rely on others for your happiness. My happiness never comes from just friends. I'm real happy just by myself.

On Age and Attitude

"Books can't damage people but they can be inappropriate. The reader's emotional development has to be taken into account. An eight-year-old who is a very good reader might have no trouble reading a particular book, but it might not be appropriate for her in terms of her development."

—PAM SACKS

"It's a mistake to create set patterns—that this happens at this stage and another—because it's not necessarily true. These things don't happen for everybody on the same time line and in the same sequence. We're always trying to measure ourselves: are we doing what's right at this point. Well, it may be right for another mother and daughter at another point."

—SUSAN MCGEE BAILEY

"During those nine-to-twelve-year-old years, mothers really need to be open and listen to what daughters have to say, and not get upset if the daughters don't seem to be as devoted to them as they would like them to be. Listen to their goals and their dreams. Because if a mother has some goal set in her mind, and it isn't the daughter's goal, that's when the daughters rebel. That can escalate and damage the relationship. I like to tell mothers to just keep an open mind, allow your children to express themselves, and talk with them."

— BERTHA WATERS

"It's wonderful sharing books and sharing a real love of reading. I have a daughter who's eight and a son, eleven, and I started reading to them when they were two days old. It was a wonderful way to share a wonderful experience from my own childhood, and to know that my children have that."

— HARRIET MOSATCHE, PH.D.

"Sex discrimination, race discrimination—I'd rather let them know it's out there, and sit down and talk about it."

— CONNIE PORTER

MOM: But a child...

MOM: Even for a child. I think some children are just loners.

MOM: I think it's okay to be a loner, but there's something about being loved that makes you able to be alone and be comfortable. And I think—in fact, I hope the girls think in terms of love being what really matters. The long hair is not going to give you the happiness and satisfaction that I think we all want. Even Patty Ann wanted that more than anything. But she thought the way to have it was to be attractive physically. But it didn't work.

MOM: I think that was my concern. That's why I wanted to press the issue a little bit... .

At this point one of the girls introduced a new question, and the discussion moved on to the subject of the grandmother characters in the books. They discussed how those characters were similar and how they were different. And how their cooking had been a part of the characters. Then one of the girls asked again: "Why do you think Patty Ann had an eating disorder?"

GIRL: I don't know.

GIRL: Because she wanted to be Ms. Perfect and so she thought that if she ate all this food and stuff, she would get fat, so she just wanted to make herself stay thin so she wouldn't get fat.

GIRL: I agree—Patty Ann didn't want to be fat. She would put her finger in her mouth and throw up her food because she didn't want to be fat.

GIRL: I think it was partly that. But I also think she didn't really like the food and she didn't want to upset her mother.

GIRL: You can eat something you don't like so much and just forget about it—you don't have to throw up.

GIRL: She didn't want to be fat and also she might not have liked the food. It could have been both.

That discussion forged ahead into many other aspects of the characters and the stories, none of them getting back to Patty

Ann's troubled state of mind.

Taken as a whole, the discussion touched on lots of issues—friendship, happiness, peer pressure, self-esteem—that brought out thoughtful responses from the girls. But their attitude toward that eating disorder was rather matter-of-fact. It was clear from their comments that most of them dismissed it as an extreme act of dieting by a girl who simply "didn't want to be fat." Or didn't like the food. Neither response suggested they had any understanding of eating disorders or the kinds of issues that foster that kind of self-destructive behavior. And they didn't pick up on our explanations and pursue those thoughts.

Later, when I thought about their comments, I realized that the girls actually were making a very strong statement; it just wasn't about the subject we had in mind. It was about themselves, their level of experience in the world, and their readiness to discuss the subject. They were ready to talk about happiness, motivation, and the ups and downs of grades, looks, friendships and grandmothers—things they understood well from experience. But they weren't ready to talk about the psychology of eating disorders.

"We don't always agree on things. There was a book where people were feeling like one character was a mean little girl—the girls saw her as someone who thought she was better than everyone else because she got good grades and wasn't 'part of the crowd.' But I compared her to myself at that age and I could relate her situation to things that had happened to me. I asked the girls if she reminded them of anyone they knew, maybe someone from school."

LESLYE FRASER

The mothers might have wished the girls had reached a moment of clarity and insight about the subject—some one-line moral to the story to carry through adolescence. They didn't, but that didn't mean the discussion fell short of any mark. In fact, the

AGE AND ATTITUDE:
READERS AND WRITERS

Two books we think of now as classic children's literature raised a few questions when they were new. *Charlotte's Web* told the story of a pig saved from slaughter by a kind and literary spider. In *Stuart Little*, a caring, intellectual mouse sets out in search of a missing friend. Author E. B. White's letters share some thoughts he had about his young readers:

Letters from E. B. White, author of *Charlotte's Web* and *Stuart Little*

October 22, 1952

... So far, *Charlotte's Web* seems to have been read largely by adults with a literary turn of mind. I have had only a sprinkling of childhood reaction to the book... and will not know for a little while how it sits with the young. I have a step-grandchild named Caroline Angell who is a quiet little girl of about five. She listened attentively to the reading of the book by her father, and said: "I think there was an easier way to save Wilbur, without all that trouble. Charlotte should have told him not to eat, then he wouldn't have been killed because he would have been too thin.

Trust an author to go to a lot of unnecessary trouble.

April 18, 1961

Dear Mrs. Sanborn:

The ending of *Stuart Little* has plagued me, not because I think there is anything wrong with it but because children seem to insist on having life neatly packaged. The final chapters were written many years after the early chapters and I think this did affect the narrative to some extent. I was sick and was under the impression that I had only a short time to live, and so I may have brought the story to a more abrupt close than I would have under different circumstances. My reason (if indeed I had any) for leaving Stuart in the midst of his quest was to indicate that questing is more important than finding, and a journey is more important than the mere arrival at a destination. This is too large an idea for young children to grasp, but I threw it to them anyway. They'll catch up with it eventually. Margolo, I suppose, represents what we all search for, all our days, and never quite find.

girls had talked candidly about their ideas. Without lecturing, the moms had woven in a few pieces of information about eating disorders, including that they are a sign of something else that needs attention. And the conversation included discussion about other normal, but sometimes stressful, aspects of everyday life. That was, perhaps, the most important message our girls needed to hear that day: Life can get complicated, self-destructive behavior needs attention and it's okay to talk with their mothers about any and all of it.

A collection of folktales brought us to a discussion of marriage, and then to another question involving men and women and the division of power and strength in the world. The girls said they felt women had power, but when the talk turned to specifics, they got giggly.

GIRL: Okay. The questions are: Pretend you're old enough to get married. What are some qualities you think would make a perfect man?

MOM: Whoa! (*laughing*)

MOM: Anyone want to go first?

MOM: Is it that you all don't know what qualities would make a perfect man, or is it the thought of getting married—why are you all hiding your faces?

GIRL: He'll be nice and kind of sweet.... .

RAISING COMPETENT GIRLS:
ONE SIZE DOES NOT FIT ALL

Age isn't the only dividing line for maturity and perspective among girls. The standards for self-worth by which our girls measure themselves often are different from girl to girl, depending on a lot of issues including racial or cultural influences, according to the study "Raising Competent Girls: One Size Does Not Fit All."

Sumru Erkut, at the Wellesley Centers for Women, and her colleagues—Fern Marx, Jackie Fields and Rachel Sing—evaluated information from 161 adolescent girls about what qualities they felt were important for a girl to like herself.

Most of the girls put a lot of stock in "physical appearance, behavioral conduct and scholastic competence"—good looks, good behavior and good grades. In one particular category called "global self-worth"— meaning how a girl measured her overall personal worth—African-American girls measured their worth more by grades; Caucasian girls measured it by physical appearance and behavioral conduct; Chinese-American girls measured by behavioral conduct and close friendship; and Latina girls measured their global self-worth by physical appearance and behavioral conduct.

LISTENING:
HEARING THE GROWING GIRL

As girls get older, as they leave those preschool years and hit the six-to-eight-year-old range, what becomes more and more important is being able to listen to them and give them the space to be people—to be themselves. Girls, up to the age of twelve, are extremely clear about who they are and what they want.

As they go into adolescence, they become more sophisticated in how they express those feelings, and it's important for us to listen. Sometimes it's hard for mothers. In some ways we feel we know them so well, but their minds are developing and they're getting older, and sometimes we forget to give them the room they need to be able to question and change. We keep assuming they're the same little person they were when they were younger. It doesn't mean there aren't ways they are the same. There's just much more going on for them that's different, and it helps to be able to approach who they are with curiosity and not with certainty.

—ELIZABETH DEBOLD

GIRL: And thoughtful.

GIRL: And patient.

MOM: What else? Anybody?

GIRL: Well, I'd probably want the person to have a job. But not a garbage collector.

GIRL: A big house... (*all laughing*)

MOM: Handsome?

GIRL: Yeah.

MOM: Well, wait a minute, now. Let's talk about this. What is "personality"? Why do you say you don't want a garbage collector?

GIRL: He'll come home smelly.

MOM: Not necessarily. He probably showers and changes at the plant.

MOM: What if he owns the company? You know, you have to work your way up through the ranks. Maybe he started out as a garbage guy and moved up to own the company. What about that?

GIRL: (*groaning*) Mo-o-o-o-om. (*all laughing*)

MOM: Do you all want to get married? This is just fun—do you want to get married?

GIRL: No.

GIRL: Yeah.

MOM: Why?

GIRL: I don't know.

MOM: Well, why did you say yes?

GIRL: 'Cause I like kids. No, I'm not going to get married. I'm going to adopt them.

MOM: And you—you don't want to get married either?

GIRL: Nope.

MOM: Why?

GIRL: I want to have a profession.

The discussion moved on to other aspects of the books under discussion. In one folktale, a man and a woman have to choose between their desire for power and their desire for strength. The woman chooses power, while the man chooses strength, a decision he later regrets.

MOM: Which would you rather have—power or strength?

GIRL: I would rather have power because then you'd be smarter.

GIRL: I'd rather have power because then you can be strong and do other things.

MOM: Do you think that women are more powerful than men?

MOM: Why are you all acting so embarrassed when you talk about men having power? I know you have strong opinions. Can't you share them?

MOM: Let me ask it in a different way. If you believe women have more power, why haven't we ever had a woman president of the United States?

GIRL: Because it's too much work. You have to work all the time. And you don't have time for yourself.

MOM: Anybody else?

GIRL: Maybe it's because women think they can't do it. So they don't want to bother with it.

MOM: But you all believe you have the power. So, therefore, you might try... (*no response*) Is it individual power you think you have? And does that translate into collective power for women as a group? Or do you think women individually are powerful within their own homes?

GIRL: Huh?

MOM: Do you think that you're powerful by yourselves or do you know how to put that power together and do something as a whole group?

GIRL: If you set your mind to it you can do both.

SENSITIVE SUBJECTS AT ANY AGE

Is there an "appropriate" age for reading the language of hate or violence? Should we draw our girls' attention to books that portray pain, sadness and grief when there seems to be too much of it already on the pages of the newspapers and the TV screens in our homes?

Every mother has to reach her own conclusions. Some books you'll simply pass by, maybe for now, maybe forever. Other books may have important stories to tell—stories you'd like to share with your daughter—but they include words or images with which you are uncomfortable or find inappropriate. Some of the "classics" present this problem: They have powerful stories to tell but sometimes include insensitive or derogatory references to people. Some modern fiction—just like the movies—includes language or scenes we may not feel our daughters are ready to encounter without explanation.

> *"Our Mother-Daughter Book Club has been everything I thought it might be, and maybe a little more. I didn't imagine in the beginning that the girls would bring about the depth of discussion that they have."*
>
> ALICE THOMAS

Life itself is more painful than fiction at times, deserving of explanations, yet still unimaginable for some children growing up today.

"When we drive back to see our family in South Carolina, where I grew up, I talk to my daughters as we pass landmarks and I take them back to see the houses we lived in," says Joyce. "When we go to the Rexall drugstore there, I explain how on Saturday afternoons black people like us didn't go 'uptown' because that's when the Ku Klux Klan was there soliciting and passing out literature. It wasn't a safe place for us. I can tell they regard it as fictional. They hear me, but they don't. You want to share with them, but you don't want to scare them."

GIRL SCOUT SURVEY:
WHO WE ARE AND WHAT WE THINK

The most pressing worries of girls may not be what adults would predict.

For the most part, the problems that the average Girl Scout worries about most for herself are not the problems that adults and the media often focus on, i.e., drugs, sex, violence. This same finding resulted from a national study on beliefs and moral values of boys and girls across the country, when children were asked to select the one problem that most worried them. This does not mean that Girl Scouts do not worry about these other issues. Rather, like most girls their age, their most urgent concerns have to do with their home and school lives.

The problems Junior Girl Scouts (ages eight to eleven) worry about most are family problems: lack of love and care from parents, problems in their family, or physical abuse of kids. In contrast, Cadette (ages eleven to fourteen) and Senior Girls Scouts (ages fourteen to seventeen) worry most about the pressure to do well in school, and Senior Girl Scouts report the added worry of what to do with their life.... .

The pressure to do well in school seems to be the problem most consistently felt by all girls in this study, with about 40 percent of all girls worrying about this a lot and about 20 percent worrying at least somewhat.

The majority of girls in this study feel they are pushed a lot to "do the right thing." Girls feel pressured to:

* Obey parents and teachers (67 percent)

* Not to take drugs (63 percent)

* Get good grades in school (62 percent)

* Prepare for the future (53 percent)

Girl Scouts who are black feel even more pushed to do these things than other girls do. As girls get older, pressures to get good grades and prepare for the future are felt even more strongly.

Just over one-third of Girl Scouts feel pushed a lot to be popular and "fit in" with their peers. (Hispanic and Cadette Scouts report more acute feelings of pressure than others.)

Older girls (Cadette and Senior Girl Scouts) were asked about how pushed they feel to engage in at-risk activities, such as having sex, drinking, smoking cigarettes and taking drugs. The vast majority of girls say they feel hardly any pressure to engage in those activities...very few (4 percent) said they felt pressured to take drugs.

When girls don't know what is the right thing to do, they are most likely to turn to their parents for advice. This is true of all ages, although Junior Girl Scouts are more likely to seek parental advice (77 percent) than Cadette Girl Scouts (56 percent) and Senior Girl Scouts (51 percent). Other sources of advice girls reported are friends, who become increasingly important as girls get older, siblings and other relatives, and then teachers or coaches.

GIRL SCOUTS OF THE U.S.A., *Who We Are, What We Think,* 1990

The Mother-Daughter Book Club provides a comfort zone for meeting the troubling fictions, as well as the facts, of life. Shared reading at home and group discussion provide an excellent opportunity to explore *what* the author wrote and *why*. We can talk about the influence of culture and how it sets the scene for the story—whether in books or life. We can talk about cultural pressures on the individual—that's peer pressure in our daughters' lives—and the qualities an individual can bring to life that enable her to survive and thrive whether it is a character in a book or the reader herself.

"In the beginning, after we'd read our books, we were surprised at how many people answered the questions and really got into the questions. I thought it was fun."

MORGAN

The moms in our Mother-Daughter Book Club dropped some books from consideration after we previewed them within our mothers' group. Other books had passages or scenes that we felt were stretching our comfort zone, but for a good cause. Reading the story with our daughters at home, we were able to put mature or troubling aspects of a story into a context, and identify historical or cultural influences at work in the plot or dialogue.

We talked about the reasons an author might write about painful or disturbing things in a book for a young reader. We talked about the author's choice of words or events used in the story. By the time we got together for our group discussion, both mothers and daughters had defused these issues and were ready to share these thoughts and others in stimulating discussion.

WHEN TO START A MOTHER~DAUGHTER BOOK CLUB

It took me nine years with Morgan to reach a point where I felt the need and the inspiration to organize a Mother-Daughter Book Club. You don't have to wait that long. Nor should you feel that you've missed your chance if your daughter is older.

Any age is a good age to read with our daughters. When is the best time to start a Mother-Daughter Book Club? That depends upon your interests, your daughter's interests and the kind of club you envision.

For us, that nine-to-twelve age group seemed like such a perfect fit for a number of reasons. By this age, the girls have developed solid reading and listening skills, and are developing critical thinking skills and the confidence to contribute to group discussion. They're able to discuss abstract ideas to some extent, and enjoy expressing their opinion as a way of communicating. They're thinking deeper than they let on sometimes, but then they're willing to share those thoughts if you give them a little nudge. The discussion is always lively!

"It's helped me at school, too. When I read to the class I recognize and understand words that I did not know before we started the club. Reading at home has allowed my mom to work with me to help me pronounce and recognize words better."

ASHLEY S.

A group of first graders isn't going to pursue the same kinds of books and discussion you could reasonably expect to share with a group of fourth graders. That doesn't mean you can't have a Mother-Daughter Book Club when your daughter is in first grade. You just need to organize one that provides an age-appropriate response to her little-girl reading skills and interests *and* seems appealing to the mothers involved.

For instance, you might plan to have mothers and daughters read short novels together—with mom doing a lot of the reading aloud. Or you might decide to make the club meeting into a read-aloud storytime followed by twenty minutes of discussion. You couldn't expect a six- or seven-year-old child to lead a group discussion by herself. But she could enjoy other aspects of hosting the meeting, help come up with discussion questions or select the read-aloud story for that meeting. With sensitivity to younger chil-

SIMPLE STORIES:
UNIVERSAL THEMES FOR ANY AGE

Some books are good for discussion at any age because they have a quality that produces interest—something that lends itself to looking at the story from the character's perspective.

Appelemando's Dreams, by Patricia Polacco, is a wonderful example. It's about a a sleepy, drab little village where there lives a young boy who dreams incredible and colorful dreams. The adults in the town think he's a "slow," do-nothing kind of kid, but his four friends see his dreams. His dreams come right out of the top of his head—they're very colorful—and at one point cover the town, buildings and everything. The townspeople think the kids have painted the town and are very upset with them. The children, feeling very dejected, run off to a dangerous forest. When they become afraid they're lost, they ask Appelemando to dream. At the urging of his friends the boy starts to dream, and his dream fills the sky. The townspeople, who really do love the children, are able to find them by following the dream. At the end of the story, the townsfolk acknowledge the importance of dreams, and the village becomes a vibrant place—a changed place because of a young boy's dreams.

You can ask some of the same questions of any readers, any age, and you'll hear a different discussion depending on where they are developmentally and in life experience:

✷ Why do the adults see the dreamer as a do-nothing? Do you agree or disagree with them?

✷ Why do his friends appreciate him?

✷ What does it mean to be a friend?

✷ The dreamer is different from his friends. How are you different from your friends?

✷ How did the dreamer feel when his friends loved him but the adults didn't understand him? How did he feel about himself?

✷ How would you feel in a situation in which you agreed with your friends, or they supported you, and your parents didn't?

✷ How do your friends influence you? How do you influence them? What can you do if your friends are doing something you don't agree with?

✷ Think about solutions. How could you deal with the problem to avoid a crisis or confrontation?

✷ Why did the children run away? How could a problem like this be solved without running away?

✷ What do we mean when we say "dream"? What makes a sleeping dream different from a daydream? How can dreams become expectations? What are your dreams or expectations for the future? What can you do to make those dreams real?

—BONNIE DIAMOND
Language Arts Specialist

dren's patterns of thought and activity, you might start the meetings with a story and discussion, shifting the playtime to afterward.

As you consider adaptations to make for the younger and younger child, when the idea starts sounding more like a mother-daughter play group than a book discussion group, do your play group. Simply include a read-aloud story as part of it. Have some silly fun talking about the characters in the story or what they did. Whether you call it a Mother-Daughter Book Club or just an age-appropriate good time, our daughters are never too young to enjoy books, stories, and us.

Some books, too, are good for nearly any age, or good reading again and again as we age. Sometimes it's because the themes are so beautifully simple and beautifully told that they can be appreciated by readers of any age. Other times it's because the story is so rich, and the author so gifted a writer, that we experience the book differently as we come to it at different times in life.

"I've read *The Thorn Birds* every year for fifteen years," says Alice. "I never tire of it; it's like going back home again. There are characters I saw in a certain way when I was younger, and now that I'm where I am in my life I see them in a different light. Every time I read it I see more, different things. I look forward to reading it each year."

When Joyce was in second grade, her teacher read *Charlotte's Web* to the class. "That year I checked it out and read it again and again and again," Joyce says. "It's still one of my favorite books of all time. It introduces the life cycle and it introduces death to kids, but shows how people can approach that calmly and with dignity. As a child, I was sad when Charlotte, the spider, died. But I was delighted that Charlotte lived on in her children, and I wondered what life was like for them."

"Sometimes I read after dinner, or if I get up early I just take a flashlight and read in bed."

MAYA

What about older daughters? There's no doubt in my mind that mothers and their teenage daughters can enjoy a Mother-Daughter Book Club tremendously, and that there's a real need for the kind of sharing and communication that goes on in the cir-

MOTHER~DAUGHTER BOOK CLUBS AT ANY AGE

Within the context of age, interests, skills, experience and maturity, the steps for organizing a mother-daughter book club remain the same:

✳ **Think about the kind of group** you'd like to see develop. Identify any special objectives you have in mind. Avoid anything that feels like school, from kindergarten to college.

✳ **Keep in mind any age-related aspects** of the mother-daughter relationship that are likely to influence how daughters or mothers experience the reading, the discussion or the social aspects of the mother-daughter book club.

✳ **Discuss your idea** with your community or school librarian, bookstore adviser or others who have special experience that might help you adapt ideas to fit the needs of the daughters and mothers in your group—whatever their age.

✳ **Talk to prospective members** about the idea. Find a core group. Select some books to get started. Give it a try!

✳ **Establish realistic expectations** for the group and stay flexible about details.

Remember, the point of a mother-daughter book club is to share books, ideas and fun. If it doesn't feel right, change it.

cle. However, as they move along into their teen years, the girls get busier and absorbed more completely in their own lives and blossoming independence. Their interests change—sometimes by the hour. And pretty predictably, I'm told, their interest in socializing with mothers fades fast. Still, I'm an optimist. And a realist—I do have a teenage son and know many teens and their mothers through church and other community activities.

I believe it can be done.

The two biggest challenges to developing the club with teenagers are the issues of time and "cool."

Time is a flexible thing in terms of Mother-Daughter Book Club meetings. Make them quarterly, or plan them for vacation breaks.

Cool is another thing. Cool is what the Mother-Daughter Book Club needs to be in the eyes of your teenage daughter, and anything organized by moms is not likely to qualify. I'd suggest asking for outside help. Look to the youth group coordinator at your church or synagogue, or the local community center, for advice or involvement as a facilitator. These or other individuals who enjoy a special rapport with teens can make *anything fun*— even a book club discussion with *mothers*!

There is life after the teen years, and I know for a fact that some adult daughters and mothers pass books back and forth between them—often by mail if they don't live close by—and they enjoy chatting about them on the phone.

I don't think there's a bad time to start a mother-daughter book club. There's no age limit on our desire to have strong, loving relationships, and there's no age limit on the fun of doing it through shared reading and discussion.

GROWING TOGETHER: ACROSS MILES AND YEARS

Change is a natural part of growth, so anticipate change in your mother-daughter book club as time goes by. You may change

Books to Grow On

Coming-of-age stories for girls and their moms (that might inspire you to write your own):

A Thousand Pieces of Gold, Ruthanne Lum McCunn

A Tree Grows in Brooklyn, Betty Smith

Anne Frank: The Diary of a Young Girl, Anne Frank

Catherine, Called Birdy, Karen Cushman

A Wrinkle in Time, Madeleine L'Engle

Diary of Latoya Hunter: My First Year in Junior High, Latoya Hunter

The House on Mango Street, Sandra Cisneros

—PEGGY ORENSTEIN, AUTHOR
SchoolGirls

Here are four of my favorites:

Oh, The Places You'll Go!, Dr. Seuss

The Story of Ruby Bridges, Robert Coles

Ella Baker: A Leader Behind the Scenes, Shyrlee Dallard

Thank You, Dr. Martin Luther King, Jr., Eleanora E. Tate

—MARION WRIGHT EDELMAN, FOUNDER AND PRESIDENT
Children's Defense Fund

the focus of your reading selections to reflect new group interests. You may change the time you meet to accommodate other commitments. Even the group itself is bound to change over time, as this family moves away or that person can no longer fit the reading or meeting time into her schedule. But you invite new members to join the group. You explore new territory on the bookshelf. You continue to share your reading list with the one who leaves, and share conversation through phone calls, letters or e-mail. And through it all, mothers and daughters keep reading and talking together.

When we talk about our group, we talk about it as a group that will go through life. I believe it will. I believe, too, that every time we meet and talk, the embrace we give to ideas is felt in a way that will stay with each of us through life. The experience shapes us at any age. We're never too young or too old to enjoy the benefits.

ENDNOTES

★ Think about a girl's interests, maturity, her reading skills and confidence level rather than just her chronological age when determining your book selections.

★ The mother-daughter book club provides a comfort zone for talking about all kinds of subjects—even sensitive ones.

★ Any age can be a good age to read with our daughters or to start a club.

★ Think about asking an outside discussion leader to help organize a mother-daughter book club for teen daughters.

CHAPTER NINE

USING THEMES
TO GUIDE CHOICES

A people's literature is the great textbook for real knowledge of them.

The writings of the day show the quality of the people

as no historical reconstruction can.

—EDITH HAMILTON, *Preface to* The Roman Way

Rebecca & Linda Chastang

My name is Rebecca. I am eleven years old. I like to play soccer. I play on a "select" team. Although I am a defensive player, last week I kicked the only goal in the game that put us in a tie for the championship. That felt great!

I like to read and write. I was invited to serve on the vestry of the National Cathedral School. That means that I help plan chapel services for the students. I want to be a surgeon when I grow up.

I am nice. I am thoughtful, sensitive, responsible, well organized, trustworthy and trusting. I work hard. Fairness and justice are very important to me.

My all-time favorite book is *Harriet the Spy*. I liked it because Harriet reminded me of myself. She liked to read. I like to read. She liked to write. I like to write. Although I don't spy on people, I think it would be fun to do so.

My mother's name is Linda Earley Chastang. She is almost shorter than me. She tries to be funny, and she is very smart. She lets my brother's and my friends hang out at our house. She takes us fun places. We saw the United States Women's Soccer Team go to the gold!

My mom is a lawyer, and she used to be a professor, too. She stopped working in an office so she could spend more time with us at home. My mom reads, quilts and talks on the phone. She plays board games, goes to lots of meetings and goes walking with her friends in the morning. She likes to sleep in the hammock at our beach house.

My mother and I don't disagree about much. The thing we do disagree about is clothes. I don't like to wear what she wants me to wear.

My mother loves me and takes care of me. I think I am very lucky to have her as my mother.

Every mother-daughter book club is a "special interest group" in the best sense of the word. Each mother and daughter there has a special interest in sharing quality time together and exploring the world of ideas through books and group discussion with other mothers and daughters.

There are other ways to use special interests, or themes, to open up new opportunities for learning and experience through your mother-daughter book club. You might use a theme as the basis for selecting books to read for a period of time—focusing on historical fiction, biography or poetry, for instance. Or you might use a theme as the cornerstone in organizing your mother-daughter book club—inviting friends with whom you share a particular interest or life experience.

The mother-daughter book club can round out our daughters' education without sending them to another classroom. Schools tend to educate in general; they don't educate to the specifics. They can't fill some of the voids or instill your values and the things you care about. One way to do that is through reading. There are so many books that reach any interest area, it's fun picking and choosing. And the search is ever-evolving. The theme you pick initially may not be theme you stay with indefinitely.

Themes allow us to make special connections, fill a void or bring a balance to our life experience through the books we choose or the people with whom we read and discuss our books.

THE THEME-BASED CLUB:
BRINGING A BALANCE TO LIVES

Two particular themes first motivated me to organize our Mother-Daughter Book Club. One was the mother-daughter relationship and my desire to find ways to expand the common ground for friendship between Morgan and myself. I thought of the other mothers I knew who felt the same need. We all agreed that a mother-daughter book club might help strengthen our relationships by providing some connections through literature, discussion and the sharing of our own stories. And the special time together could bring some balance to our lives, which felt increasingly pressured by outside commitments and expectations.

My other objective was to bring together a group of mothers and daughters who shared our African-American heritage and the desire to explore the diversity of African-American literature and lives in a full way. That couldn't happen in school or in most of the girls' after-school activities, where the composition of the group and the curriculum or activities reflected other, generalized cultural perspectives.

Many parents today, regardless of their particular ethnic or religious identity, are looking for ways to help their children preserve their cultural roots as they grow and establish themselves in a multicultural society. That can be quite a challenge. Our homes are in one place, our work in another. Grandparents and other extended family may be scattered around the globe. We're all so busy with demands of the day, within the culture of the present tense, that there aren't many opportunities to casually reflect on the experience of generations past. Our children don't learn enough about their own family's heritage through the school system, and this is another way to bring in that history and culture without making it burdensome on top of their academic load. A mother-daughter book club gives you a special circle of affirmation, a place and a "family" of partners with whom you explore and celebrate these cultural connections.

"I read for fun. I like to read a lot of Native American folklore, tales and things. I like how they have a free and perfect world there and I like the descriptions of the places in the woods."

JAMEXIS

Others may find those connections easy or close enough, and wish instead for a group that includes a more diverse collection of friends. Or friends-to-be: a community-based mother-daughter book club could expand your circle of friends among mothers and daughters who simply share a love of books, discussion and friendship.

GETTING IDEAS FOR
STUDY THEMES AND BOOKS

Whether your group wants to focus on a special interest for a few meetings or as an ongoing exploration, you'll find many sources of great ideas and materials in your community. Pick a topic and ask for suggested reading, book-related activities, author information or theme-related activities. Use some networking skills to build your list of resources. Always ask contacts if they can suggest any other people, organizations or other resources for you to try: For starters:

✶ **Ask bookstore contacts**

✶ **Ask librarians**

✶ **Ask teachers**

✶ **Ask insiders**—clergy, scholars, professionals, counselors or social workers, athletes, etc.

✶ **Call museums or other cultural centers** in your area or elsewhere. Many have education departments or staff members who would be glad to help you on your way.

Keep all contact names and suggestions in your club notebook or filed away. You may want to turn to them again, or help someone else on the same quest!

EXPLORING SPECIAL INTERESTS
THROUGH LITERATURE

Whatever brings your group together, theme-based reading selections can add a special dimension to your literary explorations and discussions. The key is to stay flexible and use themes to broaden your reach—not limit it.

When our group organized, we thought we'd focus completely on African-American authors and literature. There's such a wealth of it and, historically, it wasn't included in school programs or even on the shelves at most bookstores. Our first year was exciting with our discovery of the rich array of voices from the black community. In addition to vibrant historical fiction, we discovered wonderfully written stories depicting more modern times. Universal themes played out in the context of the lives of girls who were of African-American, Puerto Rican, Jamaican, and other cultures of color.

Then we branched out. The girls elected to read about girls from other cultures. The selections we read included *Homesick: My Own Story*, by Jean Fritz, about an American girl who was born in China and came to the United States at age twelve; *Julie of the Wolves*, by Jean George, the story of a native Alaskan girl; and *The Friends*, by Rosa Guy, a story set in Harlem, which touches on class issues confronting two Jamaican sisters when their family relocates there.

Our book list, by meeting month, for our first two years, reflected the evolution of our interests:

Year One, 1995–96:
The Ear, the Eye and the Arm, Nancy Farmer (November 1995)
The Man in the Ceiling, Jules Feiffer (December 1995)
Charlie Pippin, Candy D. Boyd (January 1996)
The House of Dies Drear, Virgina Hamilton (March 1996)
Cousins, Virginia Hamilton (April 1996)
The Shimmershine Queens, Camille Yarbrough (May 1996)
Her Stories, Virginia Hamilton (June 1996)

Year Two, 1996–97:

The Mystery of Drear House, Virgina Hamilton (September 1996)

Julie of the Wolves, Jean Craighead George (October 1996)

The Friends, Rosa Guy (November 1996)

Homesick: My Own Story, Jean Fritz (December 1996)

Life in the Ghetto, Anika D. Thomas (January 1997)

Time Cat, Lloyd Alexander (February 1997)

Mama's Girl, Veronica Chambers (March 1997)

Rites of Passage, Tonya Bolden (April 1997)

Regardless of the composition of your group, themes are a fun way to add a little structure to your reading plans and enjoy the three-dimensional framework it provides for discussion as you read and compare the books. There's so much good literature, it's a treat to look at the ways you can track a theme through fiction, poetry, biography and nonfiction.

The process of picking a theme and selecting books within that theme provides more opportunities for mothers and daughters to talk about ideas. When our girls pick the subject, they enjoy the feeling of having chosen the direction for the club's reading. The mothers then can scout out books that satisfy both the girls' interest in a subject and the mothers' interests in subjects we'd like to bring into discussion with them.

I think most mothers want to raise their daughters to become strong, responsible women. We want to teach them the values we hold dear—self-reliance, faith, compassion and generosity—without hit-

> ### BOOKS TO GROW ON
>
> *Anne of Green Gables,*
> Lucy M. Montgomery
>
> *The Secret Garden,*
> Frances Hodgson. Burnett
>
> *Harriet the Spy,*
> Louise Fitzhugh
>
> *Dragonflight,*
> Anne McCaffrey
>
> *The Autobiography of Miss Jane Pittman,*
> Ernest Gaines
>
> *When Hitler Stole Pink Rabbit,*
> Judith Kerr
>
> —PAMELA WOOD,
> HEAD OF MIDDLE SCHOOL
> Friends Seminary, New York, New York

MIX AND MATCH: EXPLORING THEMES THROUGH BOOKS AND MORE

Pull from the full world of literature to explore a theme topic! Consider novels, nonfiction books or essays, short stories, poetry and plays. Enrich your reading experience with related activities such as movies, video documentaries, author contact or field trips to historic and other sites of interest.

Sample Special Interest Theme: ANIMALS/NATURE

BOOKS:

Black Beauty by Anna Sewell

Charlotte's Web by E. B. White

The Secret Garden by Frances Hodgson Burnett

Venus Among the Fishers by Elizabeth Hal and Scott O'Dell

Rachel Carson's biography

POETRY:

The Earth Is Painted Green: A Garden of Poems About Our Planet,
edited by Barbara Brenner

Refreshments: Fresh fruits, vegetables, grains, and edible flowers

Centerpiece: "Season's Greetings" any time of year
with a table centerpiece made of recycled sticks, bark, stones,
leaves, moss, etc. from yard or park.

Nature Scavenger Hunt: Compile list of words from book
describing things in nature, and find as many as possible
in the backyard or neighborhood park.

Field Trip: Go to a nature preserve, zoo or animal shelter, or
talk with a naturalist, ranger or community educator.

ting them over the head with it all. Selecting books by theme provides the basis for a balanced mother-daughter partnership: The girls' interests can provide the direction; the mothers can provide the books.

Think of themes as a visit to a big museum. It's a wonderful way to explore the unknown, satisfy your curiosity, expand your knowledge and enlighten your perspective. But you don't have to stay in one place until everyone's begging to leave. Visit, go elsewhere, come back another time.

There's no limit to the themes you can identify and explore. For example, a group with a particular interest in the arts might start with a biography of an artist's life, discussing the personal qualities the artist brought to life's challenges and opportunities. Another book might be chosen as a way to explore a particular era or culture and the contribution it made to the world of visual or performing arts. A third selection might be one that had been made into a movie. The group could read the book, see the movie and discuss how the story was translated from one form to another.

There are so many views from which to explore the world, and so many views of the world to explore. Some

> ## BOOKS TO GROW ON
>
> ### Literature of Science
>
> Astronomy: *Coming of Age in the Milky Way*, Timothy Ferris
>
> Biology: *The Double Helix*, James Watson
>
> Chemistry: *The Periodic Table*, Primo Levi
>
> Geology: *Rising from the Plains*, John McPhee
>
> Physics: *Surely You're Joking Mr. Feynman!*, Richard Feynman
>
> Medicine: *The Youngest Science*, Lewis Thomas
>
> Psychology: *The Man Who Mistook His Wife for a Hat*, Oliver Sacks
>
> Nature: *The Immense Journey*, Loren Eiseley
>
> and, for good measure,
>
> *A Natural History of the Senses*, Diane Ackerman
>
> —ROBERT HAZEN, AUTHOR
> *Science Matters*

perspectives for creating either a theme-based group or list might include:

    ✳ **Cultural**—Multicultural, African-American, Hispanic, Asian, Jewish or other ethnic identities

    ✳ **Religious**—explore your own or the diversity of religions in the world

    ✳ **Life challenges**—divorce, illness, disability, loss, grief and recovery

Brainstorm for ideas within your group. Take the "I wish" list of subjects or styles or authors your group would like to read, and consider the many options, including book-related activities. Here are a few for starters:

    ✳ **An author:** Read several books by the same author, looking for opportunities to mix novels, nonfiction, poetry, if possible. Always check for a biography. Quite a few authors write for young adults and young children—read and compare the styles and themes. Ask local bookstore or library advisers about any authors who might live in the area and be available to talk with your group, or about planned author visits to your community.

    ✳ **Diaries:** Look under historical fiction for these treasures.

    ✳ **Plays:** There are

BOOKS TO GROW ON

I've focused on secret adventurers:

The Egypt Game,
Zilpha K. Snyder

Calamity Jane's Letters to Her Daughter/Martha Jane Cannary Hickok
Calamity Jane

From the Mixed-Up Files of Mrs. Basil E. Frankweiler,
E.L. Konigsburg

Annie on My Mind,
Nancy Garden

Gone-Away Lake,
Elizabeth Enright

The Borrowers,
Mary Norton

—ELIZABETH WHEELER

THEMES FOR ALL SEASONS, ALL PEOPLE

One of my favorite books, especially good for the nine-to-twelve age group, is *In the Year of the Boar and Jackie Robinson,* by Bette Bao Lord. In the story, it's 1947 and a Chinese girl moves from China to Brooklyn, renaming herself "Shirley" after Shirley Temple. In Brooklyn she finds a true melting pot of people from every ethnic and racial group. She grows to love baseball, and Jackie Robinson is her hero.

The way the author handles the aspects of tradition, cultures and ethnicity is extraordinary, and it models for our children the theme of diversity as something to celebrate.

The chapters are named by month, so I often tie that in to the start of the new calendar year and read it with children in January. That, in turn, ties in to Martin Luther King Jr.'s birthday, which gives the discussion a good starting point on the theme of prejudice, whether it's about race, religion or the clothes kids wear to school. The book also introduces Jackie Robinson, a world-known figure "bigger than life," but having some of the same problems that ordinary people have. Some questions with which to explore prejudice:

✷ What do you think when you see someone dressed in a way that you see as unusual or different?

✷ In what ways do you form opinions about people? By their looks or language? By their age or grade? How do you form opinions about people when you don't know them?

✷ **When you know someone,** what are the qualities about them that make them special to you?

Change, and how we cope with it, is another theme in *In the Year of the Boar and Jackie Robinson*, and a very important part of life today. Our children can learn skills for coping from watching us and reading about others' struggle with change. Some discussion questions:

✷ **What do you think about change?** What kinds of changes do you like? What kinds of changes do you dislike? Can a change that's hard become one that's good? How?

✷ **How do you cope with change,** and how do your parents help you cope with change? How important is it to have help and support during change?

✷ **What kind of changes have you experienced** and how did you cope with them? This might be changing schools, moving, family changes, events or illness that change our lives.

—BONNIE DIAMOND
Language Arts Specialist

many plays written for young people. Some are in paperback-style booklet collections and include adaptations of classics as well as newer plays. The Pleasant Company also publishes packets plays featuring its American Girl characters. Check with a librarian for help in finding plays.

* **History:** Pick an era and read a couple of historical fiction books and a biography of a notable woman of the time. Consider a trip to a local museum, a movie depicting the era or a documentary video.

* **Leadership:** Ask a helpful librarian to suggest a few novels in which girls' leadership qualities are portrayed in a real-life setting. Add a biography of a woman leader in history. Consider inviting a local community leader to talk with your group about her life and personal history.

EXPERIMENTING WITH THEMES: BIRDS, BEES & BLUNDERS

Whenever you pick a book with a particular theme in mind, be ready for a lesson of another kind—always inspired by the reality of girls' thinking. We learned our lesson with an ill-fated motherly scheme to address "coming of age" issues within the comfort of the book club circle.

During our mother-time talks we had shared our feelings of trepidation at the looming need to discuss issues of sexuality with our soon-to-be-teen girls. Frankly, we felt like wimps. We thought that we—and the girls—might find courage and comfort in having the conversation within our circle, using a book as the focus of attention. We made two mistakes and one inspired decision.

The mistakes came first. First, over muttered protest by the girls, the mothers picked the book. It was a good book, a highly respected nonfiction volume written to introduce girls and women to their bodies and issues of sexuality in a clear and positive way. Second, over a background noise of quietly desperate objections by the girls, we assigned the book and one of the mothers cheerfully volunteered to host the meeting. It was put on our roster for a meeting a few months off.

Within about a week, the mothers were on the phone to each other. It wasn't working. At home, individually, the girls' desperation had turned to defiance. They'd read it, but no way were they going to talk about it in a group. Even the girls who had read it before wouldn't admit it to the other girls.

Then came the inspired decision. We mothers agreed among ourselves to just drop it as a group activity. At the next meeting, when we turned to picking books for the future, I simply mentioned in passing that we all were reading the book, and talking about it at home, but that we wouldn't plan to use it for group discussion after all. We didn't criticize or tease the girls for feeling the way they did. We treated the change in a matter-of-fact way, leaving it with a note of encouragement to mothers and daughters to read and chat about the book together. And then we moved on.

The lesson? I count four, at least: Don't be afraid to try new ideas. Listen to your girls and respect their feelings. Speak up when something isn't working. And be willing to change your mind.

BOOKS TO
GROW ON

Books I have enjoyed as a child
and lower school librarian:

The Secret Garden,
Frances Hodgson Burnett

King of the Wind,
Marguerite Henry

Where the Lilies Bloom,
Vera Cleaver and Bill Cleaver

A Begonia for Miss Appelbaum,
Paul Zindel

Yolanda's Genius,
Carol Fenner

Homecoming,
Cynthia Voigt

The Little Fishes,
Erik Haugaard

A Wizard of Earthsea,
Ursula K. Le Guin

— PHOEBE BACON,
SCHOOL LIBRARIAN
National Cathedral School, Washington, D.C.

Embracing the World
Through Books and Discussion

Parents—black, white, Latino—need to talk about differences, about what makes this country what it is today. We may not all agree on the interpretations, but we all need to talk about what's happened. You can't talk about the meaning of a voters' proposition about affirmative action if you don't understand the history of what was done to black people.

I've always liked to read historical fiction, even as a girl. History is a continuous story of people. I wanted that to come through in the Addy books. The people were slaves, but you're talking about somebody's mother and father. There were moments of heroism and humor and joy. They didn't just sit around wringing their hands. Every day was not spent gnashing teeth. To portray them that way is to reduce people's lives to that.

A mother's love or a father's love is what life always has been about, and it doesn't change in slavery. In Addy I wanted to make sure that there is something in their lives that is joyous. Something that speaks of hope.

Historical fiction can really teach a young person, who has no way of contacting the past, to know about the past. When I go to schools and bring things it gives the children a way of entering another time period and using their imaginations. It gives them a chance to go back and compare their lives with the lives of people a long time ago.

And I hope it gives them a sense of perspective on how life has changed in this country and how much they take for granted. And there should be a sense of pride, no matter who you're reading about—a little Jewish girl emigrating, a black child coming out of slavery, a white farm girl on the prairie—they're getting a hope and appreciation for what it took to build a nation. It wasn't one person's story or one group's story.

I have to think that if there's any way for this country to survive, it will be in finding a common ground we can share. All around the globe, all around, there are many thousand examples of what happens when you separate and hate.

—CONNIE PORTER

Support Groups:
Mothers, Daughters & Special Needs

No life is ordinary. But some lives contain particular events or circumstances—divorce, death, chronic illness or other stressful conditions—that add an extraordinary measure of challenge for mothers and daughters. That challenge can bring them together or push them apart, and sometimes both. Quite often, mother and daughter are in need of emotional support from outside the family as well as from within their relationship.

For those who have challenges in common, a mother-daughter book club provides the emotional equivalent of a room with a view. The group offers a "safe haven" of acceptance and understanding, while the books and discussion can add new perspective to stimulate fresh thinking.

For instance, a group of single moms and daughters might find a special comfort zone in their own mother-daughter book club. Typically, the single mother and her daughter face so many challenges—emotional, practical, financial. In a group setting, there is affirmation and encouragement from others facing similar challenges. When brought into a circle of caring others, that experience can translate into a wealth of insight and understanding.

The group might look for books that portray nontraditional families and individuals with challenges in common. Or it might shift the focus away from the familiar and look to biographies for compelling life stories or to poetry for powerful emotional expression.

The club concept can easily be adapted to groups in which any "significant other" adult in a girl's life is her partner for reading and discussion. Those possibilities are endless and offer a structure for sharing and strengthening a special relationship.

SPECIAL CONSIDERATIONS:
SO MANY WAYS TO LOVE A BOOK

Amy is not going to be able to read lots of books, but it's why I think it's so important to see each of our children as individuals. She carts around this big bag of books. Many people might assume a young woman with her developmental difficulties would have no interest in books, as she reads at only a third-grade level. But she finds great pleasure in books. She likes to read whatever she can find around. Some of her joy is just being able to say the words, not necessarily putting the whole story together.

When you think about it, a book, whether you open and read from beginning to end, or open it and read here and there, or just look at the pictures you remember, it is a wonderful thing to have because you can put yourself in a different place for a while.

—SUSAN MCGEE BAILEY

(Susan Bailey's daughter, now twenty-six, has some physical handicaps and is developmentally and physically disabled.)

READING: A CONSTANT THEME
IN MOTHERS' LIVES

When I was school age, the word *theme* meant term papers, essay questions on tests and long-winded lectures from classroom teachers—bless them all. Today when I hear the word, I think about books and lives, and the threads that run strong through them, giving texture and definition.

Among the women and girls in our Mother-Daughter Book Club, reading itself is a theme that has shaped and inspired our lives as far back as most of us can remember.

My mother has always been a constant reader; I can't imagine her without a book in her hand, or her travel bag, on the table or—if nowhere in sight—on her mind! That mental picture has turned out to be worth a thousand words—or books, to be more precise. When my brothers and I went to help her declutter the basement, we were overwhelmed by the number of paperback books we found! We packed up dozens of bags of books to give to charities, and, of course, my mother kept dozens more she wasn't ready to part with.

My bond with books goes way back, my mother tells me. She named me Shireen, inspired by what she thought was a beautiful name of a character in one of those paperback novels. What a lasting gift from a reading mother to a loved daughter.

Our Mother-Daughter Book Club is full of reading moms who are rich with happy memories of their own mothers, and of reading. We took some time to reflect on that theme in our lives, and the memories made a wonderful sharing experience.

"My earliest memories of my mother are of her reading, always," Kathie says. "Books, magazines, articles. We could be going on a trip in the car and we'd ask a question and she'd always know the answer—and she could tell you where she'd read it, too. She still reads all the time."

Alexis remembers being a "voracious reader" as a child. "I would read under this walnut tree at my grandmother's house. Other times I would read in my room. I would close the door, and

I would get so engrossed in my book I wouldn't even come down for food," Alexis says. "I would read for pleasure. Books took me so many places. I always felt I would see the places when I got older, but reading about them ensured that at least I saw them in my mind."

Reading was and remains important in her parents' lives, too, she says. "My mother and I are very close, and when I was young, I watched her—she was always there with the family. Most of her reading was recipes and the newspaper. I would watch her read, and being the inquisitive one, I would ask what she was reading. She would always put the book in front of my face and say, 'Here, you read it to me.' I think she enjoyed hearing my voice. When I go visit them at home even now, I read to them. My father and mother both love *National Geographic*, so I'll read that to them and we talk about it."

Reading together in a home with busy mothers comes up again and again.

"I come from a family of seven children and we lived with my mother and father in a three-bedroom, one-bath home," says Alice. "I would use books to escape. I remember sitting out under our apple tree and reading every single Laura Ingalls Wilder book. Then and now, when I find an author I really like, I read all the books that author has written, and then I move on.

"When I was young I read a lot. I read the autobiographies, like Helen Keller's. I read a lot of The Bible—I read The Bible from cover to cover one year when I was about ten. I read a lot of Nancy Drew. It was more recreational than anything. I used to imagine myself as the characters in some of the books, and I would use those books to get ideas about writing and I'd write little stories about those characters, putting myself and my family into the book.

"My mother always loved, and still loves, reading, but she just didn't have much time," Alice says. "With seven children, her hands were always busy, but I would sit down and read with her. And that's how we would read together."

Mothers and Daughters:
Themes Forever

No matter what the general theme of our book selections, our interest in the theme of mothers and daughters remains a constant. We always take note of the ways girls and women are portrayed in the stories, the way the author uses them in a book's cast of characters, the qualities that the author assigns them. We compare their book life with our own life experiences to explore points of difference or common experience.

That exploration of the world and our own lives together—through books, discussion and sharing—is the one theme that stays the same in a mother-daughter book club. It's one interest none of us will ever outgrow!

ENDNOTES

* ✸ Use special interests, or themes, as a fun way to add a bit of structure to your reading.
* ✸ Use themes to broaden your reading and discussion experience.
* ✸ Brainstorm theme ideas such as cultures, religions, or life situations within your group.
* ✸ Whatever your special interests, keep the theme of mothers and daughters a constant in your club's readings and discussions.

CHAPTER TEN

BEYOND THE BOOKS

When you think about it, we don't really learn by just listening.

We learn by thinking, and by doing.

—ELLEN SILBER

TIFFANY & WINNIE DONALDSON

Hi, my name is Tiffany Kristina Donaldson. I'm eleven years old and have eyes so brown you can't even see the pupils. When I smile you can see the reflection of the light on my braces. My hair is so frizzy it looks like I have tight curls all over—that's just me!

Sometimes in the morning I can be cheerful and sometimes I'm the mad, grumpy type. My parents and I live in a condominium in northwest Washington, D.C., and I have a room of my own with everything but cable TV.

I read and swim a lot. I've been on a swim team for three summers. I don't really like sports, but I do like to play tennis. I especially like to collect things. I love my American Girl doll, and I love to collect colorful pens, interesting spoons and some sparkling stickers. I also have a big collection of coins. I have taken dance lessons for eight years, piano lessons for four years and started violin lessons last year. I've been a Girl Scout for six and a half years. My favorite foods are pizza and Cherry Garcia ice cream.

My mother's name is Winnie and she works on "the Hill"—in Congress. She's worked in presidential campaigns and congressional offices for a long time. She and my dad talk about politics a lot. He is writing a book about the civil rights movement of the 1960s. My mom is also my Girl Scout leader, so we spend a lot of time doing fun things together, and I think that's good.

I love to read, but it used to be almost always Goosebumps books. I loved them even more than TV! I like fantasy and surprise—on my birthday I even asked my mom to hide my presents around the house so I could find them. It was fun! Our reading club is fun, too. My favorite books lately have been *Tuck Everlasting, The Lion, the Witch and the Wardrobe* and *The Wolves of Willoughby Chase*. One of my favorite authors is Mildred D. Taylor—I especially liked *Roll of Thunder, Hear My Cry*.

It was a dark and stormy night. The girls crept through the dim, secret passageway, looking for an escape. They checked their tattered map and located the wall panel that was supposed to fall open and let them run out to safety. Together, they pressed into the panel.

"It won't budge! We're trapped!"

They pushed harder. The panel seemed to push back! They pushed again. And again. Suddenly, the panel gave way and the girls tumbled out—laughing and squealing and scrambling to catch the jokester on the other side—one of the girls' older brother!

He had stationed himself on the outside of the cardboard box tunnel as they'd crept through it and had held the escape panel firm for that extra moment to add a genuine element of surprise to the great escape.

Our Mother-Daughter Book Club would never forget its adventure of escape through the "underground railroad" the hosting daughter had created in her family's basement. Nor would we forget the book that took us there, *The House of Dies Drear*, by Virginia Hamilton, the story of a family and a house haunted by its past as a Civil War era safe house for those fleeing slavery.

Good books are a treasure chest of ideas. The stories themselves are the gems we enjoy first through reading and discussion. But when we look more closely within the stories, they sparkle with detail about history, foods, and the events and accessories of

---

BOOKS TO
GROW ON

Annie John,
Jamaica Kincaid

To Kill a Mockingbird,
Harper Lee

Having Our Say,
Sarah and Elizabeth Delany

Member of the Wedding,
Carson McCullers

Jacob Have I Loved,
Katherine Paterson

Night,
Elie Wiesel

The Good Earth,
Pearl Buck

Bless Me, Ultima,
Rudolfo Anaya

The Hundred Dresses,
Eleanor Estes

—AMY SCHROTH, HEAD
OF ENGLISH DEPARTMENT
The Madeira School, McLean, Virginia

everyday life. Every facet of the book—the story, the author, the era in which it was written—as well as any creative descendants of the book, such as movies, plays, museum exhibits, visual art or other stories, offer shining opportunities for fun and learning.

BOOK ACTIVITIES:
REACH FOR YOUR SENSES!

There are enough lessons in life that we learn the hard way. When there's a choice, I think learning should be as fun as possible.

The Girl Scouts have known that for a long time, and used that belief to shape their programs for success. "Not surprisingly, we have learned that girls' perspective is that Girl Scouts is, first and foremost, a place to have fun and share friendships," says a survey report by the Girls Scouts of the U.S.A. "The more they enjoy their experience, the more likely they are to remain in Girl Scouting. Achievement—through badge, patch and award programs—is also important to many girls. But it is important to remember that learning and development can only take place in an environment that girls truly enjoy."

When children are very young, they learn primarily by playing. When they get a little older, they learn by doing, which includes playing, acting, planning, building, cooking, designing, sewing—you name it—and still aims for a good time.

At this preteen age, a book becomes meaningful in one way when it connects with their intellect. It becomes memorable in a

> *"Anything that brings people together to discuss a common experience, whether it's a book or movie or having been to the same play or event, offers an opportunity to understand the same thing but know it differently, to take different things away from the same experience."*
>
> SUSAN MCGEE BAILEY

dramatically different way when it connects with their senses and feelings. In the Mother-Daughter Book Club, our shared reading and wide-open discussion of each book help us connect with the characters, the setting, the history and the author.

Book-related activities also can bridge a gap between individual learning styles. Some children learn best by reading, some by listening, some by discussing. And for some, "hands-on activity," as it's called in the schools, is the way they take an experience in.

Whatever our individual learning style may be, book-related activities are another wonderful way to enlarge our experience of the books. Book-related activities offer the girls an opportunity to be creative, each in her own way. The activity is planned by the host daughter and mother, and adds to the feeling of leadership each girl enjoys when it's her turn.

When the group read *The House of Dies Drear*, Holly took to her basement and put together cardboard boxes to make a segment of an "underground railroad" escape hideout like that depicted in the book.

"I thought hosting would be burdensome and that it would be difficult to find interesting things for them to discuss and do," Alice says. "Then when it was our turn, Holly and I discussed what we could do to make our discussion interesting and make the book come alive. She chose the topic, she chose the menu for that day. She turned our basement

> ### BOOKS TO GROW ON
>
> *Little Women,*
> Louisa May Alcott
>
> *The Hobbit,*
> J. R. Tolkien
>
> The Nancy Drew series,
> Carolyn Keene
>
> *A Wrinkle in Time,*
> Madeleine L'Engle
>
> *A Tree Grows in Brooklyn,*
> Betty Smith
>
> *Chronicles of Narnia,*
> C. S. Lewis and
> Pauline Baynes
>
> *All Creatures Great and Small,*
> James Herriott
>
> *I Capture the Castle,*
> Dodie Smith
>
> *Bridge to Terabithia,*
> Katherine Paterson
>
> *Zlateh, the Goat, and Other Stories*
> Isaac B. Singer
>
> —ROBIN ROBERTSON,
> HEAD MISTRESS
> Emma Willard School,
> Troy, New York

Do-It-Yourself Activities
Bring Stories Alive

Books are a wonderful way to learn about so many things. You don't have to stop with reading the story. Whether it's about how laundry was done, or about crop rotation, or other aspects of life for characters in the book, once you start thinking you start learning.

That's part of the value of any book. The experience of the research and activity takes on a life of its own.

In *The World of Little House* we explore the world of Laura Ingalls Wilder's Little House books and one of the points we wanted to make comes through in thinking about how people lived. People did things differently then. For instance, today, when you see craft demonstrations the focus is always on how to make things that are quick and easy.

The characters from the Little House books—and they are very true to life, all based on real people—did things in a very deliberate and caring way. They didn't mind that it took time. It was part of their entertainment and a way that they spent time.

When you see Ma giving the girls work to do in the dugout house, they're stringing buttons. Laura and Mary would string and restring those buttons, arranging them in different ways. How many children would do that now? But it's very appealing to think about it, how they spent time, concentrated, had fine motor skills. Laura was making a sampler with a needle and thread when she was four, Mary was making a quilt at five.

They were doing some pretty sophisticated things as children.

Sometimes people romanticize the "old days," or fantasize about living in a simpler era past, when life was easier. We don't want to burst anybody's balloon, but we want them to know that life was pretty hard for these people and it shows a portion of their character that they were able to persevere through a lot of hardship.

Doing an activity to bring the stories home really helps children. It gets them involved in the story a little bit more and it becomes an experience to remember. Children sometimes need a little bit of a hook to start their learning experience, especially with history. Cooking something they've read about and remember, or making something, or growing something, is always a helpful connection. Our goal is to help them relate to the classic books and want to know more.

—CAROLYN STROM COLLINS, COAUTHOR
The World of Little House

storage room into an underground railroad. She made maps, and for food we made what she thought slaves might have packed to travel: fried chicken and biscuits, raw vegetables, chocolate cake. She set the agenda, made all the questions. She did an incredible job. I was very proud of her."

Long after the meeting was over and her basement was straightened up, that underground railroad lives on in our memories.

Later we read Hamilton's sequel, *The Mystery of Drear House*, and hosts Maya and Joyce chose to put us all in Jeopardy!—the game, that is. Mothers and daughters squared off in this rapid-fire question-and-answer game based on details in the book. It was a tie-breaker, and the girls beat us to that last answer. They reveled in their victory. So did we!

"It was really fun," Maya says. "And then we were thinking about what the prizes could be and we got some bookmarks from the Smithsonian."

Trivia or mother-daughter Jeopardy!-style games can be used again and again for a good time. They help us celebrate the details of the books we read, and no matter how fierce it becomes, the competition is the best kind.

When we read *The Friends*, by Rosa Guy, we contacted the author to see if she might accept an invitation to be our special guest at our book club meeting. She accepted, along with her god-daughter, Kathe Sandler, who had made a film of part of the *Friends* story, and we made arrangements to have our meeting in a room at the Smithsonian's Center for African American History and Culture. The girls were able to see the film and discuss aspects of the story with Rosa Guy.

"It was really, really interesting to get to meet Rosa Guy," says Brittney. "We got to ask her questions and see the movie—it was great!"

Making the Connection
to Books—by Hand

Tips for Planning Book-Related Activities

✷ Pick ideas that interest the girls.

✷ Think about ways to adapt them to make them age appropriate for interest and skill.

✷ Aim for simplicity. Good projects don't have to be complicated.

✷ Aim for authenticity. Try to use materials that the character would have used at that time and place.

✷ Involve your daughter in collecting the materials.

✷ Reread a portion of the book where the activity is described.

✷ Organize all materials; get enough to allow for mistakes.

✷ Encourage girls to express their own creativity in any project.

✷ Be patient. Small motor skills improve with practice, not pressure.

✷ Acknowledge the effort each girl puts into her work, regardless of her skill level.

—CAROLYN STROM COLLINS

IDEAS FOR ACTIVITIES:
THE BOOK'S THE THING

Every story offers images we can use to taste, touch, see, smell or hear the story in a special way. Other aspects to explore include the author and the historical context for the book. Even the story itself—the language or details about characters, plot and setting—make good material for games.

⁎ **Think about field trips.** A museum, movie, community exhibit or other site may offer a special perspective on a book. Take your urban children to the countryside to experience a rural story setting. Take your suburban children to the city to see the rows of brownstones or skyscrapers that frame a character's life. A bus or train ride, or even a nature walk around your neighborhood, can be a special experience if it relates to the book.

⁎ **Think about authors.** Ask a librarian for help in locating information about the author—biographies or magazine articles, for instance. Call or write to the publisher to find out whether the author plans to visit your area on a promotional tour or lives in your area and might be willing to talk with your group. If not, consider writing to the author.

⁎ **Think about history.** Explore the historical setting for the story or the author's life. Museums are wonderful, but they're just one way to access history. Closer to home, books of historical photographs can add to the enjoyment of a story. Invite the mothers and daughters to come "dressed for the occasion"—in clothing reminiscent of the era. Or a simple activity from the book—the "old-fashioned way"—can be eye-opening.

⁎ **Think about books.** Have some fun with simple art or craft activities. Invite the girls to illustrate their favorite scenes and see if your community or school library would welcome a display. Make bookmarks or decorate canvas tote sacks or T-shirts to reflect your mother-daughter book club interests.

Taking Stories
Beyond the Books

We were on vacation last summer and waiting in a downtown area for a carriage ride, and there was a little girl sitting reading *Julie*, the sequel to the book we'd read in the group, and Maya had read them both. My shy child says to this little girl, "Do you like that book?" And they started talking about the books! Anywhere you go, you can use books as a way to learn about people and share ideas, and she's learning that.

—JOYCE YETTE

A SPECIAL MEETING,
A SPECIAL AUTHOR: ROSA GUY

Rosa Guy is the award-winning author of *The Friends*, a trilogy, and other works, including the recently published *The Sun, the Sea, a Touch of the Wind*, a book she describes as "vaguely autobiographical." Mothers and daughters had read *The Friends*, and were delighted to learn that Ms. Guy's god-daughter, professional filmmaker Kathe Sandler, had produced a segment of her aunt's award-winning novel for film.

Ms. Guy and Ms. Sandler joined us for a special meeting, where we viewed the film segment together and enjoyed a relaxed round of discussion afterward.

Her thoughts after her visit:

"I was delighted with it, delighted with the fact that the young people knew the book and had wonderful questions to ask. One often has to read books more than once to come up with good questions. I was delighted. Here was a roomful of all of them having read the book, and it wasn't school, it wasn't required reading."

Her thoughts about her work, about literature, girls and mothers?

"I just write from my experiences and my belief in people. Whether I write about girls or boys, I write with the belief that people, if they get to understand each other, there can be love for each other whoever they are.

"I grew up mostly in Trinidad; then I have lived in Harlem and the Bronx, Africa, England, Switzerland and Haiti.

"I didn't have a mother. I was orphaned. My mother died when I was very young and of course I always missed her and always projected what I would expect from a mother through my work, you know. So there is a sensibility there that comes from my being orphaned. All these things must have a particular effect; it comes through somehow.

"I was sort of a loner, part of a very small family and didn't have a lot of friends. I read extensively. All the books I read have left impressions on me because, number one, around that time they didn't have books segregated into categories—adult, adolescent, children. Fairy tales were for the very young, and then there was the rest. I did read the fairy tales, and when I got to a certain age I read adult literature. Certainly some of it stayed with me—the Brontë sisters did, in English literature, and in French, the wonderful Jean Christoffe— all of these left a fantastic impression on me and they are books I cannot forget ever.

"When I was in England, in 1995, *The Friends* was considered a 'modern classic.' I was impressed; you see, when it came out—that was more than twenty years ago—it was the first book by a black author that was put on the syllabus in Great Britain's school system.

"Things that people have told me about my work is that I never talk down to children, I just talk to them.

"To mothers and daughters, to everyone, I would just say read. Get the books that are considered good literature and read. In our libraries we have Russian literature, French literature, some of the best books in the world. *Les Miserables, Madame Bovary,* without preaching they give you the feeling of the lives these people lived. That doesn't mean you have to ignore the realities of today.

"All of it is important. The more you read the more you know."

* Think about reading. Keep a running list of "wonderful words" or "phavorite phrases" from the books. Play games that make the most of recall—words, facts, descriptions, characters and quotes.

* Think about food! Look in the book for descriptions of foods or mealtimes for refreshment menu ideas. Order takeout from an ethnic restaurant that captures the cultural flavor of the story. I made a tasty chicken dish from a recipe mentioned by a character in one of our books. And when another book took us into the Chinese culture, we asked a local baker if he could duplicate a Chinese "castle cake" mentioned in the book as an elaborate construction decorated in pink icing with little silver sparkles. The cake delivered to our house on meeting day was magnificent. It was, figuratively and literally, like something out of a book.

Girls often enjoy socializing over the kitchen table with a cooking or craft activity, their minds and hands busy with something fun to make. Activities like these are another opportunity for sharing stories and laughter between mothers and daughters. The important thing about book-related activities is that they be enjoyable and that they always leave plenty of time for book discussion. That might sound obvious, but it's important to keep it in mind, especially with a group of creative, enthusiastic daughters and mothers. If the book-related craft or activity becomes so time-consuming or complex that it overshadows discussion time, it may be best to think of a different idea. And an activity *isn't* enjoyable for a mother or

---

BOOKS TO
GROW ON

Nina Bonita, Ana M. Machado
(*younger girls*)

Sarah Phillips, Andrea Lee
(*junior high, high school*)

Strawberry Girl,
Lois Lenski

I Know Why the Caged Bird Sings,
Maya Angelou

The Bluest Eye,
Toni Morrison

Amazing Grace,
Mary Hoffman

Boundless Grace,
Mary Hoffman

—CONNIE PORTER

BOOK LOVERS BRAINSTORM:
TO THE BOOKS AND BEYOND!

✳ **Go globetrotting!** Use a globe to locate the story's setting.

✳ **See the sites!** Check with the local librarian or historical society to find out if any book-related sites might be within traveling distance for your group. Consider having your meeting at the site, or planning the field trip for a day of its own.

✳ **Write to an author**—Ask your neighborhood librarian for help in locating an address for the author of a book the club has enjoyed. Ask for a volunteer from among the girls to write the club's letter to the author, sharing the group's thoughts about the book and inviting the author to write back if possible.

✳ **Cook or serve food** that reflects the era or ethnic flavor of the story, or use a recipe from the book.

✳ **Make a story-related craft**—Try to use materials and tools they would have used at the time in the story.

✳ **Lights! Action! Reader's theater!** No need to memorize—just act out a few favorite scenes using the book as your script. Take turns being the audience and the actors.

✳ **Dress up!** Come dressed in clothing reminiscent of the era.

✳ **Paper dolls**—Make story-related paper dolls from poster board and draw your own outfits to cut out from plain paper.

✱ **Story sheets**—Use 3M's poster-sized Post-it sheets to jot down the group's ideas or invite girls to draw characters or scenes to display temporarily on a wall.

✱ **Adjective Ambush**—Divide into two teams to see who can find the most number of descriptive words first to reach a target number. Write down words and page numbers on which they appear in case the challengers call a bluff!

✱ **Verb Vendetta**—Go after the action words now—remember each word has to be found in the book!

✱ **Wonderful Words**—Keep an ongoing collection of great words or phrases the girls circle during home reading and contribute at meeting. Under a heading of the book's title and discussion date, invite each contributor to write her words in the club's book herself.

✱ **Personality Parade**—Examine characters' personalities—list and discuss their positive and negative qualities.

✱ **Tabletop themes**—Create a centerpiece or table decoration that goes along with the story. The host daughter might like to use toys or items she has—dolls, miniature figurines, action figures—to set up a scene from the book.

✱ **Bookmarks**—Make bookmarks as a memento of a story. Invite each girl to draw a picture of a character or scene from the story on one side of the paper, and on the other side write the name of the book and month and year she read it. Laminate it or use clear adhesive-backed shelf paper to cover the bookmark.

✱ **Booklist bookmark**—To celebrate the conclusion of your first year of reading together, create the bookmarks, listing the title, author and date you read each book.

* **Hall of Fame**—As you read more books, continue to compare and contrast characters from different books. Enjoy an ongoing nomination process for characters, such as the most inventive, the most thoughtful, the most creative, and other categories that encourage the girls to think of qualities that make people special or memorable.

* **Critics' Choice**—Ask for a volunteer daughter to write up the group's comments about a book that was considered particularly good, and check with the school or neighborhood library about posting the book review for others to enjoy. Create an annual list to share the same way.

* **Book club scrapbook**—Create a scrapbook for the club, inviting girls to jot down their thoughts or draw illustrations about the books or the club to fill a page or two at each meeting.

* **Let Pictures Tell the Story**—Contact local library, school, community hall or nursing home to see about displaying art the girls might make illustrating a story or idea from a story.

* **Play Detective**—A hosting daughter might compile a list of riddles about characters or events in the story and begin discussion by asking the group to identify who or what she's describing.

* **X Marks the Spot**—Enjoy a scavenger hunt without moving from your seat! Invite the girls to mark in the book or on a separate sheet of paper several words from the story that describe people, places, things or feelings. If they jot the words on paper, be sure to tell them to mark where they found them. Then ask each girl in turn to name one of her words for the others to find.

daughter who feel pressured to do it, or if it strains the budget.

I am a believer in enrichment activities—the experience of seeing, hearing, tasting and touching pieces of the stories we read. The interesting thing about mother-daughter book discussion is that the discussion itself *is* an enrichment activity, an experience no museum or field trip can deliver. When we give our book discussions the right time and attention, we go beyond the books and into the stories of our *own* lives: our history, our feelings, our dreams and concerns.

That's what makes our Mother-Daughter Book Club different from every other class, program or activity we do. That's what keeps it special. That's what keeps us coming back, despite our crowded lives and calendars.

"The club started out just reading and discussing the books, then some of the mothers became real creative with ideas for fixing food to match the books—anything to create, open up and hopefully get that stick-to-it-ness," Alexis says. "When you expand outward it makes it a living book."

Whether we simply look to the book for refreshment ideas or plan a field trip, when it comes to book-related activities, if we keep mother-daughter discussion first on our list, everything else we choose to do supports it, and every meeting becomes memorable.

ENDNOTES

✷ Good books are a treasure chest of ideas for activities.

✷ Book-related activities can bridge a gap between individual learning styles.

✷ Discussion—along with seeing, hearing, tasting and touching stories—is an enrichment activity.

✷ Use the club to move beyond discussion of the books to the stories of your own lives: your history and dreams.

THE END:
WHERE NEW STORIES BEGIN

This story of our Mother-Daughter Book Club, like any story in a book, has to end a page before the back cover. But a very special and exciting part of the story only begins here. It's not a sub-plot or a sequel. It's the story that begins in another mother's heart, in another home, in another town, where the idea of a mother-daughter book discussion group takes root. Mother-daughter book clubs can flower anywhere and anytime the desire is there.

When one of Grace's friends moved to Swaziland, Grace suggested that she and her daughter start a mother-daughter book club there. They did, adopting our club's reading list as a starting point. Now we trade comments and opinions about books electronically by e-mail!

In Chicago, my writing partner Teresa Barker and her daughter Rachel, nine, both insatiable readers, organized a mother-daughter book club with friends. After a move put forty-five minutes between them and their long-time friends, the club became a way of getting together at least once a month, along with a new friend Rachel introduced to the group from her new community.

Many of Rachel's ideas, and the experience of her club, have enriched this book and given our Mother-Daughter Book Club new ideas for book-related activities. Lynae Turner, one of the friends in Rachel's club, shares our group's African-American heritage and has found a special delight in becoming a pen pal with Morgan and our club.

In reflecting on the needs of our girls, all of us have become more vocal advocates for them, and more eager to strengthen and celebrate the mother-daughter relationship. Progress comes in small steps and big ones. Any step you take toward shared reading and discussion with your daughter is a step in the right direction. Whatever you do, the rewards far outweigh the effort.

Maybe you'll organize a mother-daughter book club that

meets monthly or quarterly. Maybe you'll bring up the idea within your neighborhood or religious community and encourage someone else to organize. Maybe you'll find just one other mother and daughter with whom to share reading and book chat over hot chocolate and cookies. Maybe for now, you'll simply find the time to read with your daughter, one book at a time, and at tuck-in time, ask: "What did you think of that story?"

Whatever you do, when you do, I'd love to hear about it. Write to us at The Mother-Daughter Book Clubs of America, Inc., 6100 13th Street N.W., Washington, DC 20011.

I see our group as an evolving circle of experience. If there's a better way to do something, or an interesting way to do something, we're eager to hear about it. Joyce, Teresa and I each have six-year-old daughters and are trying to figure out how to deal with the issue of younger siblings coming up and, soon, wanting a club of their own. What to do? And we'd like to hear from those of you who develop groups with your teenage daughters— what's cool?

This circle of mothers and daughters can reach around the globe and into so many hearts and lives!

Where does it all end? It doesn't.

Let *your* Mother-Daughter Book Club story begin!

Appendices

Mother-Daughter Book Club
Simple Startups

Need a boost to get started? These simple steps will get you on your way. Keeping your club going is even easier—a mother-daughter book club generates its own energy!

Remember that the important things about your mother-daughter book club are that you enjoy reading the books, show up for meetings and take time to let discussion flow. This doesn't have to be a costly venture. It doesn't require a professional to lead discussion. And the meetings can be arranged to accommodate any schedule.

You can do this. It's this simple:

✷ Share your idea with a few friends you know well and a few you'd like to see more often.

✷ As the first hosting mother and daughter, select a book for the group to read and discuss at your first meeting. Start with a favorite of your own, or consider one of the titles and discussion guides suggested here.

✷ Set the date and time for the first meeting.

✷ At home, help your daughter plan discussion questions about the book.

✷ At your first meeting, use an icebreaker game to get started (see Chapter 3: "The Organizational Meeting: Prelude to a Great Year"), have fun with discussion and set aside time to talk about the kinds of books that interest the girls and mothers in your group. Select books as a group or invite each girl and her mother to pick a book and a date to host a meeting.

✷ Set a date and a book for the next meeting. You're on your way!

Sarah, Plain and Tall
by Patricia MacLachlan

This book is a short, strong and beautifully written story about a motherless prairie family and the emotions that envelope them when their father arranges for a mail-order bride to come for a visit—maybe to stay.

READING TIME: 1 to 2 hours, 58 pages.

DISCUSSION THEMES: Choices, change, loss, love, family. (See sample questions below.)

Book Discussion Questions:

✶ Why was Sarah willing to leave her home to marry someone she had never met?

✶ A life on the prairie was hard. Why would someone choose to live there?

✶ Imagine you are the daughter in the story. Since your mother died you have worked hard to care for your brother and run the house and the farm. How would you feel about someone new marrying your father?

✶ Why would the father send away for a bride?

✶ What was "the worst thing about Caleb"?

✶ Does Anna love her brother? How can you tell?

✶ What do we learn about Sarah from her letters to the family before she arrives? How would you have felt about her?

✶ Why does Caleb read the letters over and over again and keep them with him when he goes to sleep at night?

✶ Why does the author write that Sarah "dressed in a pair of overalls and went to the barn to have an argument with Papa"?

✶ What is the argument about? How does it end?

✱ After you get to know Sarah, what words would you use to describe her, besides "plain and tall"?

✱ Who is the "main character" in this story?

✱ As you read the book, which character do you feel the closest to?

✱ Can you tell at what time in history the story takes place?

✱ What feelings in the story might be the same if it happened today?

✱ The story was based on a true event in the author's family history. Are there any stories like Sarah's in your family?

✱ Has your family ever changed to include a new child or a new adult? How does it feel to accept someone new into your family?

Beyond the Book Activities:

NATURE'S NAMES: List names of all birds, flowers and grasses and sea life mentioned.

DRAWING MEMORIES: Draw a picture of a favorite place you enjoy or would miss if you moved away.

MOVIE: It's available on video for home viewing. Consider watching it after reading the book, but before discussion, and include in discussion comparisons of how the characters were the same or different in the book and movie.

REFRESHMENTS/FOODS MENTIONED IN THE BOOK: Stew, biscuits.

The Midwife's Apprentice
by Karen Cushman

Winner of the 1996 Newbery Medal, this is the story of a homeless young girl in medieval England who becomes an apprentice to a midwife and, in the process, discovers her own strength and intelligence, and a place for herself in the world.

READING TIME: 2 to 3 hours, 122 pages, medium length.

DISCUSSION THEMES: Growing up, self-esteem, independence. (See questions below.)

Book Discussion Questions:

✻ How do you suppose Alyce came to be homeless and nameless, and sleeping in a dung heap when the story begins?

✻ Why was she willing to work hard for the midwife when she had not worked at a job like this before?

✻ What kind of character is the midwife?

✻ Why does Alyce decide to run and hide?

✻ What does Alyce think of herself? What do others think of Alyce?

✻ When Alyce saves the cat, she speaks harshly to him. Why? How did she feel about the cat?

✻ No one was ever kind or helpful to Alyce. Without that experience, how did she know how to be kind and helpful to Edward? Why did she choose to be that way?

✻ How does Alyce change from the beginning to the end of the book?

✻ What does the midwife need that Alyce has to offer at the end of the book?

✻ Why is that important or valuable?

✻ What might Alyce's life have been like if she had not become the midwife's apprentice?

* What would life be like for a girl like Alyce today?

* If this story was set in our time, how would it be the same? How would it be different?

* How was superstition a part of everyday life in Alyce's time?

* What kinds of treatments were offered to women in childbirth that would be considered unusual today?

* In the story's setting, what kind of life might Alyce look forward to as an adult?

* What qualities about Alyce helped her succeed? What qualities were not helpful? Can a personality quality sometimes be helpful and sometimes not?

* Would you like Alyce as a friend? Why or why not?

Beyond the Book Activities:

MEDIEVAL MENUS: Collect all the names of foods in the book and pick your favorites for a medieval peasant's feast.

REFRESHMENTS/FOODS MENTIONED IN THE BOOK: Homemade bread, butter, cheese, dried apples.

The Secret Garden
by Frances Hodgson Burnett

A classic first published in 1911, this is the story of three children whose lives are entwined and transformed by the "magic" of a secret garden. Orphan Mary Lennox, returned from India to her uncle's mansion estate in Yorkshire, England, grows from a lonely and bitter child, into an eager, caring one surrounded by the beauty of nature and good country folk.

READING TIME: 5 to 8 hours, long, about 375 pages. Yorkshire dialect can be challenging, but good for reading aloud.

DISCUSSION THEMES: Change, death, hope, friendship, social class. (See questions below.)

Book Discussion Questions:

✷ What is Mary like when we first meet her?

✷ What do we learn about her mother? How do you think Mary might have felt about her parents? About herself?

✷ What is Mary's attitude about people who are different from her — in color, language or life situation? How can you tell?

✷ When she arrives at Misselthwaite Manor, what are things that Mary finds to like? How do you know?

✷ What effect does nature have on people in the story?

✷ How is Dickon's mother different from Mary's memory of her own mother?

✷ What do Colin and Mary have in common?

✷ Is Colin sick? In what way? What does he think of himself?

✷ What do you think of Mary's uncle, Colin's father?

✷ Why does Mary begin to speak the Yorkshire dialect?

✷ Do you have a quiet place you enjoy like the secret garden?

✷ If you had discovered the secret garden, would you tell anyone?

✷ Why was the garden kept "secret"?

✷ Why didn't anyone ever speak of Colin's mother?

✷ How do the characters change from the beginning to the end of the book?

✷ If you could have written one more chapter to the book, what would the characters have done next?

Beyond the Book Activities:

AROUND THE WORLD: Have a globe handy at the meeting to find India and England.

FIELD TRIP: Visit a botanical garden to look for as many of the plants named in the book as possible, or simply to enjoy a lush, cultivated garden.

MOVIE: See any of several movie versions of the book on video at home. Compare aspects of the plot and characters.

REFRESHMENTS/FOODS MENTIONED IN THE BOOK: Homemade bread, butter, raspberry jam. Or try ethnic Indian food.

(Book club discussion questions suggested by Martha Decherd, library media specialist/teacher, David Douglas School District, Portland, Oregon.)

Selected Book Lists

Caldecott Medal Winners

1996   *Officer Buckle and Gloria*, Peggy Rathmann
1995   *Smoky Night*, Eve Bunting
1994   *Grandfather's Journey*, Allen Say
1993   *Mirette on the High Wire*, Emily A. McCully
1992   *Tuesday*, David Wiesner
1991   *Black and White*, David Macaulay
1990   *Lon Po Po: A Red Riding Hood Story from China*, Ed Young
1989   *Song and Dance Man*, Karen Ackerman
1988   *Owl Moon*, Jane Yolen
1987   *Hey, Al*, Arthur Yorinks
1986   *The Polar Express*, Chris Van Allsburg
1985   *St. George and the Dragon*, Magaret Hodges
1984   *The Glorious Flight: Across the Channel with Louis Blériot*, Alice and Martin Provenson
1983   *Shadow*, Blaise Cendrars
1982   *Jumanji*, Chris Van Allsburg

Newbery Medal Winners

1996   *The Midwife's Apprentice*, Karen Cushman
1995   *Walk Two Moons*, Sharon Creech
1994   *The Giver*, Lois Lowry
1993   *Missing May*, Cynthia Rylant
1992   *Shiloh*, Phyllis R. Naylor
1991   *Maniac Magee*, Jerry Spinelli
1990   *Number the Stars*, Lois Lowry
1989   *Joyful Noise: Poems for Two Voices*, Paul Fleischman
1988   *Lincoln: A Photobiography*, Russell Freedman
1987   *The Whipping Boy*, Sid Fleischman
1986   *Sarah, Plain and Tall*, Patricia MacLachlan
1985   *The Hero and the Crown*, Robin McKinley
1984   *Dear Mr. Henshaw*, Beverly Cleary
1983   *Dicey's Song*, Cynthia Voigt
1982   *A Visit to William Blake's Inn: Poems for Innocent and Experienced Travelers*, Nancy Willard

Coretta Scott King Book Award Winners

1996   *Her Stories: African American Folk Tales, Fairy Tales, and True Tales,* Virginia Hamilton

1995   *Christmas in the Big House, Christmas in the Quarters,* Patricia McKissack; *The Creation,* James W. Johnson

1994   *Toning the Sweep,* Angela Johnson; *Soul Looks Back in Wonder,* Tom Feelings

1993   *The Dark-Thirty: Southern Tales of the Supernatural,* Patricia McKissack; *Origins of Life on Earth,* David Anderson

1992   *Now Is Your Time! The African-American Struggle for Freedom,* Walter D. Myers

1991   *Road to Memphis,* Mildred D. Taylor; *Aida,* Leontyne Price

1990   *Long Hard Journey,* Patricia McKissack and Frederick McKissack; *Nathaniel Talking,* Eloise Greenfield

1989   *Fallen Angels,* Walter D. Myers; *Mirandy and Brother Wind,* Jerry Pinkney

1988   *Mufaro's Beautiful Daughters,* John Steptoe; *What a Morning,* Bryan Ashley

1987   *Justin and the Best Biscuits in the World,* Mildred P. Walter; *Half a Moon and One Whole Star,* Crescent Dragonwagon

1986   *The People Could Fly,* Virginia Hamilton; *Patchwork Quilt,* Valerie Flournoy

1985   *Motown and Did,* Walter D. Myers

1984   *Everett Anderson's Goodbye,* Lucille Clifton; *Mama Needs Me,* Mildred P. Walter

1983   *Sweet Whispers, Brother Rush,* Virginia Hamilton; *Black Child,* Peter Magubane

1982   *Let the Circle Be Unbroken,* Mildred D. Taylor; *Mother Crocodile,* Diop Birago

1981   *This Life,* Sidney Poitier; *Beat the Story: Drum, Pum-Pum,* Bryan Ashley

1980   *Young Landlords,* Walter D. Myers; *Cornrows,* Camille Yarbrough

1979   *Escape to Freedom,* Ossie Davis; *Something on My Mind,* Tom Feelings

1978   *The Africa Dream,* Eloise Greenfield and Cole Byard

1977   *The Story of Stevie Wonder,* James Haskins

1976   *Duey's Tale,* Pearl Bailey

1975   *The Legend of Africania,* Dorothy Robinson and Herbert Temple

1974   *Ray Charles,* Sharon B. Mathis and George Ford George

1973   *I Never Had It Made: The Autobiography of Jackie Robinson,* Alfred Duckett

1972   *Seventeen Black Artists,* Elton C. Fax

The Mother-Daughter Book Club Expanded List

(African-American titles from which the girls chose the books we read.)

Arilla Sun Down, Virginia Hamilton

Come a Stranger, Cynthia Voigt

Down in the Piney Woods, Ethel F. Smothers

Edith Jackson, Rosa Guy

Fall Secrets, Candy D. Boyd

Freedom Songs, Yvette Moore

Gifted Hands: The Ben Carson Story, Ben Carson and Cecil Murphey

A Girl Named Disaster, Nancy Farmer

The Glory Field, Walter D. Myers

Grand Mothers: Poems, Reminiscences, and Short Stories About the Keepers of Our Traditions, Nikki Giovanni

Growin', Nikki Grimes

Letters from a Slave Girl: The Story of Harriet Jacobs, Mary E. Lyons

Maizon at Blue Hill, Jacqueline Woodson

M.C. Higgins, the Great, Virginia Hamilton

Plain City, Virginia Hamilton

The Road to Memphis, Mildred D. Taylor

Roll of Thunder, Hear My Cry, Mildred D. Taylor

Ruby, Rosa Guy

The Secret of Gumbo Grove, Eleanora E. Tate

Shimmy Shimmy Shimmy Like My Sister Kate: Looking at the Harlem Renaissance Through Poems, edited by Nikki Giovanni

Sweet Whispers, Brother Rush, Virginia Hamilton

When the Nightingale Sings, Joyce C. Thomas

Zeely, Virginia Hamilton

EDITORS' FAVORITES

The following books have been recommended by an informal poll of children's book editors and publishing professionals:

Anne Frank: The Diary of a Young Girl, Anne Frank

Arthur, for the Very First Time, Patricia MacLachlan

Beauty, Robin McKinley

Beezus and Ramona, Beverly Cleary

Behind the Attic Wall, Sylvia Cassedy

Bently & Egg, William Joyce

The Best Christmas Pageant Ever, Barbara Robinson

Caddie Woodlawn, Carol Ryrie Brink

Catherine, Called Birdy, Karen Cushman

Daddy Long Legs, Jean Webster

The Daydreamer, Ian McEwan

The Diamond in the Window, Jane Langton

Dinky Hocker Shoots Smack, M. E. Kerr

The Egyptian Cinderella, Shirley Climo

The Fledgling, Jane Langton

Forgotten Beasts of Eld, Patricia McKillip

From the Mixed-up Files of Mrs. Basil E. Frankweiler, E. L. Konigsburg

Girl Goddess: Nine Stories, Francesca Lia Block

The Glass Slipper, Eleanor Farjeon

The Good Master, Kate Seredy

Half Magic, Edward Eager

Harriet the Spy, Louise Fitzhugh

Hatchet, Gary Paulson

Homecoming, Cynthia Voigt

Jacob Have I Loved, Katherine Paterson

Jason and Marceline, Jerry Spinelli

The Junkyard Dog, Erika Tamar

Make Lemonade, Virginia Euwer Wolff

Maniac Magee, Jerry Spinelli

The Mennyms, Sylvia Waugh

None of the Above, Rosemary Wells

Number the Stars, Lois Lowry

Once upon a Time, A. A. Milne

Owl in Love, Patrice Kindl

The Perilous Gard, Elizabeth Marie Pope

The Princess and the Goblin, George MacDonald

The Seven Ravens, Laura Geringer
Shabanu: Daughter of the Wind, Suzanne Fisher Staples
The Sherwood Ring, Elizabeth Marie Pope
Taste of Salt: A Story of Modern Haiti, Frances Temple
There's a Boy in the Girls' Bathroom, Louis Sachar
Toning the Sweep, Angela Johnson
Tuck Everlasting, Natalie Babbitt
Up a Road Slowly, Irene Hunt
Walk Two Moons, Sharon Creech
When I Was Little: A Four-Year-Old's Memoir of Her Youth, Jamie Lee Curtis
Winter on the Farm, Laura Ingalls Wilder
Wise Child, Monica Furlong
The Witch of Blackbird Pond, Elizabeth George Speare

RESOURCES FOR MOTHERS

Books

Altered Loves: Mothers and Daughters During Adolescence, Terri Apter (St. Martin's, 1990).

The Best in Children's Books: The University of Chicago Guide to Children's Literature, 1985–1990, Zena Sutherland, Betsy Hearne, and Roger Sutton (University of Chicago Press, 1991).

Beyond the Read-Aloud: Learning to Read Through Listening to and Reflecting on Literature, Dorothy G. Hennings (Phi Delta Kappan, 1992).

Children and Books, Zena Sutherland and May Hill Arbuthnot (HarperCollins, 1991).

Children's Literature: An Issues Approach, Masha Rudman (Longman, 1984).

Children's Literature in the Elementary School, Charlotte Huck, Susan Hepler, and Janet Hickman (Harcourt Brace College Publishers, 1993).

Children's Literature in the Reading Program, edited by Bernice E. Cullinan (International Reading Association, 1987).

Choosing Books for Children: A Commonsense Guide, Betsy Hearne (Delacorte Press, Delta, 1990).

Choosing Books for Kids: How to Choose the Right Book for the Right Child at the Right Time, Joanne Oppenheim, Barbara Brenner and Betty Goegehold (Ballantine, 1986).

Circles of Sisterhood: A Book Discussion Group Guide for Women of Color, Pat Neblett (Writers & Readers, 1996).

Comics to Classics: A Parent's Guide to Books for Teens and Preteens, Arthea J. S. Reed (Penguin, 1994).

Eyeopeners: How to Choose and Use Children's Books About Real People, Places, and Things, Beverly Kobrin (Penguin, 1988).

Failing at Fairness: How America's Schools Cheat Girls, David M. Sadker and Myra Sadker (Scribner's Reference, 1994).

For Reading Out Loud!: A Guide to Sharing Books with Children, Margaret Mary Kimmel and Elizabeth Segel (Dell, 1991).

Home: Where Reading and Writing Begin, Mary W. Hill (Heinemann Educational Books, 1989).

In a Different Voice, Carol Gilligan (Harvard University Press, 1982).

In the Middle: Writing, Reading and Learning with Adolescents, Nancy Atwell (Heinemann Educational Books, 1987).

Literature and the Child, Bernice E. Cullinan, with Mary K. Karrer and Arlene M. Pillar (Harcourt Brace Jovanovich, 1989).

Making Connections: The Relational Worlds of Adolescent Girls at Emma Willard School, edited by Carol Gilligan, Nona P. Lyons, and Trudy J. Hanmer (Harvard University Press, 1990).

Meeting at the Crossroads: Women's Psychology and Girls' Development, Lyn Mikel Brown and Carol Gilligan (Ballantine, 1993).

More Creative Uses of Children's Literature, Mary Ann Paulin (Shoestring Press, 1993).

Mother Daughter Revolution: From Good Girls to Great Women, Elizabeth Debold, Marie Wilson, Idelisse Malave (Bantam, 1993).

Mothers: Memories, Dreams and Reflections by Literary Daughters, edited by Susan Cahil (Penguin, 1988).

Narrative and Storytelling: Implications for Understanding Moral Development, Lyn Mikel Brown and Carol Gilligan (Jossey-Bass, 1991).

The New Our Bodies, Ourselves: A Book by and for Women, The Boston Women's Health Book Collective (Touchstone Books, 1996).

The New York Times Parent's Guide to the Best Books for Children, Eden Ross Lipson (Random House, 1991).

The Norton Book of Women's Lives, edited by Phyllis Rose (W. W. Norton, 1993).

Parents Who Love Reading, Kids Who Don't: How It Happens and What You Can Do About It, Mary Leonhardt (Crown, 1993).

Pass the Poetry, Please! Lee B. Hopkins (Harper & Row, 1987).

The Power of Reading, Stephen S. Krashen (Libraries Unlimited, 1993).

Raising a Daughter: Parents and the Awakening of a Healthy Woman, Jeanne Elium and Don Elium (Celestial Arts, 1995).

Raising Confident, Competent Daughters, National Coalition of Girls' Schools, (508) 287-4485.

The Read-Aloud Handbook, Jim Trelease (Viking Penguin, 1995).

Read for Your Life: Turning Teens into Readers, Gladys Hunt and Barbara Hampton (Zondervan, 1992).

Reading in and out of School, Mary A. Foertsch (National Assessment of Educational Progress, 1992).

Reviving Ophelia: Saving the Selves of Adolescent Girls, Mary Pipher (Putnam, 1994).

SchoolGirls: Young Women, Self-Esteem, and the Confidence Gap, Peggy Orenstein (Doubleday, 1995).

Shortchanging Girls, Shortchanging America, American Association of University Women (AAUW, 1991).

Smart Girls, Gifted Women, Barbara Kerr (Ohio Psychology Publishing, 1985).

Taking Books to Heart: How to Develop a Love of Reading in Your Child, Paul Copperman (Addison Wesley, 1986).

Talking to the Sun: An Illustrated Anthology of Poems for Young People, selected and introduced by Kenneth Koch, Kate Farrell (Metropolitan Museum of Modern Art, 1985).

Things Will Be Different for My Daughter: A Practical Guide to Building Her Self-Esteem, Mindy Bingham et al. (Viking Penguin, 1995).

Voices of Readers: How We Come to Love Books, G. Robert Carlsen and Anne Sherrill (National Council of Teachers of English, 1988).

Woman's Fiction: A Guide to Novels by and about Women in America, 1820–70, Nina Baym (University of Illinois Press, 1993).

The Women's Information Exchange National Directory, Deborah Breecher and Jill Lippitt (Avon, 1994).

Writing a Woman's Life, Carolyn G. Heilbrun, (Ballantine, 1988).

Writing Women's Lives: An Anthology of Autobiographical Narratives by Twentieth Century American Women Writers, edited by Susan Cahill (HarperCollins, 1994).

You & Your Adolescent: A Parent's Guide for Ages 10–20, Lawrence Steinberg Ph.D., and Ann Levine (Harper & Row, 1990).

Pamphlets/Brochures/Film

"An Introduction to Shared Inquiry," Third Edition
The Great Books Foundation
35 East Wacker Drive, Suite 2300
Chicago, IL 60601
(312) 332-5870
Web site: http://www.greatbooks.org

"Creating Readers and Writers"
"Good Books Make Reading Fun for Your Child"
"Helping Your Child Become a Reader"
"Summer Reading Is Important"
"You Can Help Your Child Connect Reading to Writing"
"You Can Use Television to Stimulate Your Child's Reading Habits"
International Reading Association
800 Barksdale Road
P.O. Box 8139
Newark, DE 19714
(302) 731-1600; (800) 336-READ
Web site: http://www.eden.com/~readthis/ira/default.htm

"Dads and Their Daughters"
"Raising Confident, Competent Daughters"
   National Coalition of Girls' Schools
   228 Main Street
   Concord, MA 01742
   (508) 287-4485
   Web site: http://www.tiac.net/users/ncgs/

"The Friends"
   Third World Newsreel
   335 West 38th Street, 5th floor
   New York, NY 10018
   (212) 594-6417
   Web site: http://www.twn.org
   (Filmmaker Kathe Sandler's adaptation of Rosa Guy's classic novel is
   available to book clubs at a special rate.)

"Helping Children Learn about Reading"
   National Association for the Education of Young Children
   1509 Sixteenth Street NW
   Washington, DC 20036
   (202) 232-8777; (800) 424-2460
   Web site: http://www.ascd.org/market/resources/other/ea65.html-

"Who We Are, What We Think"
   Girl Scouts of the U.S.A, 1990
   420 Fifth Avenue
   New York, NY 10018
   (212) 852-8000

Magazines/Newsletters/Catalogues/Web Site

Amazon.com Books
Web site: http://www.amazon.com/

Books of Wonder News
132 Seventh Avenue
New York, NY 10011
(212) 989-3270
Web site: http://www.abaa-booknet.com/alldlrs/ma/10011boo.html

Children's Bookshelf
Reading Is Fundamental (RIF)
600 Maryland Avenue SW, Suite 500
Washington, DC 20024
(202) 287-3220
Web site: http://www.ascd.org/market/resources/other/ea97.html

Children's Choices
International Reading Association
800 Barksdale Road
P.O. Box 8139
Newark, DE 19714
(302) 731-1600; (800) 336-READ
Web site: http://www.eden.com/~readthis/ira/default.htm

The Children's Small Press Collection
719 North Fourth Avenue
Ann Arbor, MI 48104
(313) 668-8056; (800) 221-8056

Chinaberry Book Service
2780 Via Orange Way, Suite B
Spring Valley, CA 91978
(800) 776-2242

Daughters
1808 Ashwood Avenue
Nashville, TN 37212
(800) 829-1088

Equity for the Education of Women and Girls
Marymount Institute for the Education of Women and Girls
Marymount College
Tarrytown, NY 10591
(914) 332-4917
e-mail: wominst@mmc.marymt.edu

Language Arts
National Council of Teachers of English
1111 Kenyon Road
Urbana, IL 61801
(217) 328-3870
Web site: http://www.ncte.org

Listening Library/Bookmates
One Park Avenue
Old Greenwich, CT 06870
(800) 243-4504
Web site: www.listeninglib.com/listlib

New Moon Network
New Moon
P.O. Box 3587
Duluth, MN 55803
(800) 381-4743

Publishers Weekly
Bowker Magazine Group
Cahners Magazine Division
249 West 17th Street
New York, NY 10011
(212) 463-6758; (800) 278-2991

School Library Journal
245 West 17th Street
New York, NY 10011
(212) 463-6759; (800) 456-9409
Web site: http://www.econoclad.com/whatsnew/slj.html -

Teachers' Choices
International Reading Association
800 Barksdale Road
P.O. Box 8139
Newark, DE 19714
(302) 731-1600; (800) 336-READ
Web site: http://www.eden.com/~readthis/ira/default.htm

Young Adults' Choices
International Reading Association
800 Barksdale Road
P.O. Box 8139
Newark, DE 19714
(302) 731-1600; (800) 336-READ
Web site: http://www.eden.com/~readthis/ira/default.htm

Organizations

American Association of University Women (AAUW)
1111 16th Street NW
Washington, DC 20036
(202) 785-7700
e-mail: info@mail.aauw.org
Web site: http://www.aauw.org.

American Library Association/Association for Library Service to Children
50 East Huron Road
Chicago, IL 60611
(312) 944-6780
Web site: http://www.ala.org

The Barbara Bush Foundation for Family Literacy
1002 Wisconsin Avenue NW
Washington, DC 20007
(202) 338-2006

Center for the Book
Library of Congress
First and Independence SE
Washington, DC 20540
(202) 707-5221
http: //lcweb.loc.gov/loc/cfbook

The Children's Book Council
568 Broadway, Suite 404
New York, NY 10012
(212) 966-1990
Web site: http://www.cbcbooks.org

The Children's Literature Center
Library of Congress
Jefferson Building, Room 100
Washington, DC 20540
(202) 707-5535
Web site: http://sc94.amelsab.gov/TOUR/libcong.html

Great Books Foundation
35 East Wacker Drive, Suite 2300
Chicago, IL 60601
(312) 332-5870
Web site: http://www.greatbooks.org

Institute for the Education of Women and Girls
Marymount College
100 Marymount Avenue
Tarrytown, NY 10591
(914) 631-4917

International Reading Association
800 Barksdale Road
P.O. Box 8139
Newark, DE 19714
(302) 731-1600; (800) 336-READ
Web site: http://www.eden.com/~readthis/ira/default.htm

The Libri Foundation
P.O. Box 10246
Eugene, OR 97440
(541) 485-8532
Web site: http://www.teleport.com/~librifdn/index.html -

The Ms. Foundation for Women
120 Wall Street, 33rd floor
New York, NY 10005
(212) 742-2300
Web site: http://www.ms.foundation.org

National Coalition of Girls' Schools
228 Main Street
Concord, MA 01742
(508) 287-4485
Web site: http://www.tiac.net/users/ncgs/

National PTA
1 IBM Plaza
Chicago, IL 60611
(312) 670-6782
Web site: http://www.pta.org/pta/issues/jobdone.htm

Wellesley College Center for Research on Women
106 Central Street
Wellesley, MA 02181
(617) 283-2500
Web site: http://www.wellesley.eduWCW/wcwhome.html

Women's National Book Association
160 Fifth Avenue
New York, NY 10010
(212) 675-7805
Web site: http://bookbuzz.com

RESOURCES FOR DAUGHTERS

Books

The Creative Journal for Teens: Making Friends with Yourself, Lucia Capacchione, Ph.D. (Newcastle, 1992).

Finding Our Way: The Teen Girls' Survival Guide, Allison Abner and Linda Villarosa (HarperCollins, 1995).

Great Books for Girls, Kathleen Odean (Ballantine, 1997).

Series of Special Interest

American Girls. Series of historical fiction featuring girls of different periods in U.S. history. Includes several titles for each character: Felicity, from the Revolutionary War era; Addy, from the Civil War era; Kirsten, a Swedish immigrant pioneer in 1885; Molly, from the World War II era; and Samantha, from the Victorian era. The American Girl collection also includes dolls, book-related materials, a magazine and other interactive activities. (Pleasant Company).

Dear America. Series of historical fiction diaries of girls, each with a closing chapter of historical illustrations, maps and information. Titles include *The Winter of Red Snow: The Revolutionary War Diary of Abigail Jane Stewart, Valley Forge, Pennsylvania, 1777,* and *A Journey to the New Worl: The Diary of Remember Patience Whipple, Mayflower, 1620* (Scholastic, 1996).

Girlhood Journeys. Series of historical fiction featuring the lives of girls of different countries. The series includes *Juliet: A Dream Takes Flight,* about a girl in medieval England of 1339; *Kai: A Mission for Her Village,* about an African girl from the Yoruba tribe in southwestern Nigeria in 1440; *Marie: An Invitation to Dance,* about a young dancer in pre-revolutionary Paris, France, in 1775; and *Shannon: A Chinatown Adventure,* about an Irish immigrant in San Francisco in 1880. Girlhood Journeys also includes dolls, book-related materials, a readers' club and other interactive writing activities. (Simon & Schuster, 1996).

The Whole World. Series of classics, unabridged, illustrated and annotated in documentary style with historical photographs, maps, and more. Titles include *Heidi,* Johanna Spryi; *Around the World in Eighty Days,* Jules Verne; *The Call of the Wild,* Jack London; *Tom Sawyer,* Mark Twain; and *Treasure Island,* Robert Louis Stevenson. (Viking, 1995).

Magazines/Newspapers

American Girl
Pleasant Company
8400 Fairway Place
P.O. Box 620190
Middleton, WI 53562
(800) 845-0005
Web site: http://www.pleasantco.com

Calliope
Cobblestone Publishing Co.
7 School Street
Peterborough, NH 03458
(603) 924-7209
Web site: http://www.cobblestonepub.com

Children's Book-of-the-Month Club Review
Children's Book-of-the-Month Club
Division of Book-of-the-Month Club
Time-Life Building
1271 Avenue of the Americas
New York, NY 10020
(212) 522-4200; (800) 233-1066

Children's Express Quarterly
30 Cooper Square, 4th floor
New York, NY 10003
(212) 505-7777
Web site: http://www.ce.org

Cobblestone
Cobblestone Publishing Co.
7 School Street
Peterborough, NH 03458
(603) 924-7209
Web site: http://www.cobblestonepub.com

Cricket
315 Fifth Street
P.O. Box 300
Peru, IL 61354
(800) 827-0227

Girls' Life
4517 Harford
Baltimore, MD 21214
(800) 999-3222

HUES
P.O. Box 7778
Ann Arbor, MI 48107
(800) 483-7482
Website: http://www.hues.net

Kid City
P.O. Box 52000
Boulder, CO 80322
(800) 678-0613

Many Girls' Voices
National Association of Independent Schools
1620 L Street, NW
Washington, DC 20036
(202) 973-9700

National Geographic World
National Geographic Society
Seventeenth and M Streets NW
Washington, DC 20036

(800) 638-4077

The New Girl Times
215 West 84th Street
New York, NY 10024
(800) 560-7525

New Moon: The Magazine for Girls and Their Dreams
P.O. Box 3587
Duluth, MN 55803
(218) 728-5507
Web site: http://www.newmoon.org

Owl Magazine
Owl Communications
179 John Street, Suite 500
Toronto, ON M5T 3G5
Canada
(416) 971-5275
Web site: http://www.owl.on.ca

Stone Soup
P.O. Box 83
Santa Cruz, CA 95063
(408) 426-5557

3-2-1 Contact
Children's Television Workshop
P.O. Box 53051
Boulder, CO 80322
(303) 614-1465

Zillions
Consumers Union
P.O. Box 54861
Boulder, CO 80322
(800) 288-7898

Organizations

Children's Book-of-the-Month Club
Division of Book-of-the-Month Club
Time-Life Building
1271 Avenue of the Americas
New York, NY 10020
(212) 522-4200; (800) 233-1066

Doubleday Children's Book Club
6550 East 30th Street
P.O. Box 6347
Indianapolis, IN 46206
(800) 688-4442

The Girl Scouts of the U.S.A.
420 Fifth Avenue
New York, NY 10018
(212) 852-8000

Girls, Inc.
30 East 33rd Street
New York, NY 10016
(212) 689-3700

Mother-Daughter Book Clubs of America, Inc.
6100 13th Street, NW
Washington, DC 20011

Troll Book Clubs
100 Corporate Drive
Mahwah, NJ 07430
(800) 526-5289
Web site: http://www.troll.com

Trumpet Book Clubs
P.O. Box 60003
Columbia, MO 65205-9888
(800) 826-0110

The Weekly Reader Children's Book Clubs
4343 Equity Drive
Columbus, OH 44216
(800) 456-8220

READING LIST BIBLIOGRAPHY

Aesop's Fables, (Brimax Books, 1994).

Alice in Wonderland and *Through the Looking Glass*, Lewis Carroll (Grosset & Dunlap, 1946).

All Creatures Great and Small, James Herriot (St. Martin's Press, 1992).

Amazing Grace, Mary Hoffman (Dial Books for Young Readers, 1991).

American Girls Collection series (Pleasant Co.).

Annabel Lee, Edgar A. Poe (Tundra Books, 1987).

Anna Karenina, Leo Tolstoy (David McCay Co., 1992).

Anne Frank: The Diary of a Young Girl, Anne Frank (Doubleday & Co., 1996).

Anne of Green Gables, Lucy M. Montgomery (Everyman's Library Children's Classics, 1995).

The Anne of Green Gables Treasury, Carolyn S. Collins (Viking Penguin, 1991).

Annie John, Jamaica Kincaid (Farrar, Straus & Giroux, 1985).

Annie on My Mind, Nancy Garden (Farrar, Straus & Giroux, 1992).

Another Country, James Baldwin (Vintage Books, 1993).

Appelemando's Dreams, Patricia Polacco (Putnam Publishing Group, 1995).

Are You There, God? It's Me Margaret, Judy Blume (Bantam Doubleday Dell Books for Young Readers, 1991).

Arilla Sun Down, Virginia Hamilton (Point, 1995).

Arthur, for the Very First Time, Patricia MacLachlan (Trophy, 1989).

The Autobiography of Miss Jane Pittman, Ernest Gaines (Bantam Books, 1982).

Baby Island, Carol R. Brink (S & S Children's, 1993).

The Baby-sitters Club series, Ann Martin.

The Bears' House, Marilyn Sachs (E. P. Dutton, 1971).

Beauty, Robin McKinley (Trophy, 1993).

The Beet Queen, Louise Erdrich (Henry Holt & Co., 1986).

Beezus and Ramona, Beverly Cleary (Camelot, 1993).

A Begonia for Miss Applebaum, Paul Zindel (HarperCollins Children's Books, 1989).

Behind the Attic Wall, Sylvia Cassedy (Camelot, 1994).

Bella Arabella, Liza Fosburgh (Four Winds Press, 1986).

Bently & Egg, William Joyce (Trophy, 1997).

The Best Christmas Pageant Ever, Barbara Robinson (Trophy, 1988).

Between Mothers and Daughters: Stories Across a Generation, ed. Susan Koppelman (Feminine Press at the City University of New York, 1985).

The Bible, ed. by Harold Bloom (Chelsea House Books, 1987).

Black Beauty, Anna Sewell (Random House Value Publishing, 1996).

Bless Me, Ultima, Rudolfo Anaya (Warner Books, 1995).

The Bluest Eye: A Novel, Toni Morrison (Alfred A. Knopf, 1994).

A Blue-Eyed Daisy, Cynthia Rylant (Bradbury Press, 1985).

Blue Fairy Book, Andrew Lang (Fine Communications, 1994).

The Bomb, Theodore Taylor (HarBrace Juvenile Books, 1995).

The Book of the City of Ladies, Christine de Pizan (Persea Books, 1982).

The Borrowers, Mary Norton (HarBrace Juvenile Books, 1991).

Boundless Grace, Mary Hoffman (Dial Books for Young Readers, 1995).

The Boxcar Children series, Gertrude C. Warner.

Breaking Ice: An Anthology of Contemporary American Fiction, Terry McMillan (Viking Penguin, 1990).

Bridge to Terabithia, Katherine Paterson (HarperCollins Children's Books, 1977).

Caddie Woodlawn, Carol R. Brink (S & S Children's, 1990).

Calamity Jane's Letters to Her Daughter/Martha Jane Cannary Hickok, Calamity Jane (Shameless Hussy Press, 1976).

The Catcher in the Rye, J. D. Salinger (Little, Brown & Co., 1991).

Catherine, Called Birdy, Karen Cushman (Trophy, 1995).

Celine, Brock Cole (Farrar, Straus & Giroux, 1989).

Centerburg Tales, Robert McCloskey (Puffin Books, 1977).

Charlie Pippin, Candy D. Boyd (S & S Children's, 1987).

Charlotte's Web, E. B. White (HarperCollins Children's Books, 1952).

The Chronicles of Narnia, C. S. Lewis and Pauline Baynes (HarperCollins Juvenile Books,1994).

Colored People, Henry L. Gates Jr. (Alfred A. Knopf, 1994).

Come a Stranger, Cynthia Voigt (Atheneum, 1986).

Coming of Age in Mississippi, Anne Moody (Dell Publishing Co., 1992).

Coming of Age in the Milky Way, Timothy Ferris (Doubleday & Co., 1989).

Corduroy, Don Freeman (Viking Children's Books, 1968).

The Country Girls Trilogy and Epilogue, Edna O'Brien (Farrar, Straus & Giroux, 1986).

Cousins, Virginia Hamilton (Putnam Publishing Group, 1990).

The Cuckoo's Child, Suzanne Freeman (Greenwillow Books, 1996).

Daddy Long Legs, Jean Webster (Puffin, 1995).

Dandelion Cottage, Carroll W. Rankin (Marquette County Historical Society, 1982).

David Copperfield, Charles Dickens (Chelsea House Publications, 1992).

The Daydreamer, by Ian McEwan (Trophy, 1996).

The Day It Rained Forever, Virginia T. Gross (Viking Children's Books, 1991).

Dealing with Dragons, Patricia C. Wrede (HarBrace Juvenile Books, 1990).

The Diamond in the Window, Jane Langton (HarperCollins, 1973).

Diary of Latoya Hunter: My First Year in Junior High, Latoya Hunter (Random House, 1993).

Dinky Hocker Shoots Smack, M. E. Kerr (Trophy, 1989).

Dinner at the Homesick Restaurant, Anne Tyler (Alfred A. Knopf, 1982).

The Double Helix, James Watson (NAL/Dutton, 1969).

Down in the Piney Woods, Ethel F. Smothers (Random House,1994).

Downright Dencey, Caroline Dale Snedeker (Doubleday, 1927).

Dragonflight, Anne McCaffrey (Ballantine Books, 1986).

Drop Dead, Julia Cunningham (Knopf, 1987).

The Ear, the Eye, and the Arm, Nancy Farmer (Orchard Books Watts, 1994).

The Earth Is Painted Green: A Garden of Poems about Our Planet, Barbara Brenner (Scholastic, 1994).

Edith Jackson, Rosa Guy (Peter Smith Publishers, 1993).

The Egypt Game, Zilpha K. Snyder (Dell Publishing Co., 1996).

The Egyptian Cinderella, Shirley Climo (HarperCollins, 1992).

Eleanor Roosevelt, Rachel Toor (Chelsea House, 1989).

Elidor, Stan Garner (Yearling Books, 1993).

Ella Baker: A Leader Behind the Scenes, Shyrlee Dallrd (Silver Burdett, 1991).

Ellen Foster, Kaye Gibbons (Algonquin Books, 1987).

English Fairy Tales, ed. by Joseph Jacobs (Alfred A. Knopf, 1993).

Fall Secrets, Candy D. Boyd (Puffin, 1994).

Finding My Voice, Marie G. Lee (Dell Publishing Co., 1994).

The Fire Next Time, James Baldwin (Random House, 1995).

The Fledgling, Jane Langton (Trophy, 1995).

The Fling, Julian F. Thompson (Puffin Books, 1996).

Forgotten Beasts of Eld, Patricia McKillip (Harcourt Brace, 1996).

Foxfire: Confessions of a Girl Gang, Joyce C. Oates (E. P. Dutton, 1993).

Freaky Friday, Mary Rodgers (HarperCollins Children's Books, 1972).

Freedom Songs, Yvette Moore (Puffin, 1992).

The Friends, Rosa Guy (Henry Holt & Co., 1973).

From the Mixed-up Files of Mrs. Basil E. Frankweiler, E. L. Konigsburg (S & S Children's, 1987).

The Gammage Cup, Carol Kendall (HarBrace Juvenile Books, 1990).

George's Marvelous Medicine, Roald Dahl (Puffin Books, 1991).

Gift from the Sea, Anne M. Lindbergh (Pantheon Books, 1991).

Gifted Hands: The Ben Carson Story, Ben M.D. Carson and Cecil Murphey (Harper Mass Market Paperbacks, 1993).

Girl Goddess: Nine Stories, Francesca L. Block (HarperCollins, 1996).

A Girl Named Disaster, Nancy Farmer (Orchard Books, 1996).

The Girl with the Silver Eyes, Willo D. Roberts (Scholastic, 1991).

The Giver, Lois Lowry (Houghton Mifflin Co. 1993).

Giving Tree, Shel Silverstein (HarperCollins Juvenile Books, 1986).

The Glass Slipper, Eleanor Farjeon (HarperCollins, 1995).

The Glory Field, Walter D. Myers (Point, 1996).

Go Ask Alice, Anonymous (Avon Books, 1991).

Go, Dog, Go, Philip D. Eastman (Random House Books for Young Readers, 1966).

Gone-Away Lake, Elizabeth Enright (HarBrace Juvenile Books, 1990).

Gone with the Wind, by Margaret Mitchell (Warner Books, 1993).

The Good Earth, Pearl S. Buck (Washington Square Press, 1994).

Good Griselle, Jane Yolen (HarBrace Juvenile Books, 1994).

The Good Master, Kate Seredy (Viking, 1986).

Goody Hall, Natalie Babbitt (Farrar, Straus & Giroux, 1986).

Goosebumps series, R. L. Stine.

Go Tell It on the Mountain, James Baldwin (Random House, 1995).

Grace, Jill P. Walsh (Farrar, Straus & Giroux, 1992).

Grand Mothers: Poems Reminiscences, and Short Stories About the Keepers of Our Traditions, Nikki Giovanni (Henry Holt & Co., 1994).

The Grass Is Singing, Doris Lessing (NAL/Dutton, 1976).

Greek Myths, Geraldine McCaughrean (S & S Children's, 1993).

Grimms' Fairy Tales, Jacob and Wilhelm Grimm (Puffin Classics, 1996)

Growin', Nikki Grimes (Puffin, 1995).

Half Magic, Edward Eager (Harcourt Brace, 1996).

Hans Christian Andersen's Fairy Tales, Hans C. Andersen (Courage Books, 1996).

Harriet the Spy, Louise Fitzhugh (HarperCollins Children's Books, 1964).

Hatchet, Gary Paulson (Aladdin, 1996).

Having Our Say : The Delany Sisters' First 100 Years, A. Elizabeth Delany, Sarah L. Delany (Kodansha, 1993).

Heartburn, Nora Ephron (Random House, 1996).

Heidi, Johanna Spyri (William Morrow & Co., 1996).

Helen Keller: The Story of My Life, Helen Keller (Signet Classics, 1988).

Her Stories: African American Folk Tales, Fairy Tales, and True Tales, Virginia Hamilton (Scholastic, 1995).

High Wind in Jamaica, Richard Hughes (Buccaneer Books, 1995).

The Hobbit, J. R. Tolkien (Houghton Mifflin Co., 1984).

Homecoming, Cynthia Voigt (Fawcett Book Group, 1987).

Homer Price, Robert McCloskey (Puffin Books, 1976).

Homesick: My Own Story, Jean Fritz (Putnam Publishing Group, 1982).

The House at Pooh Corner, A. A. Milne (Dutton Children's Books, 1991).

House of Dies Drear, Virginia Hamilton (S & S Children's, 1968).

The House on Mango Street, Sandra Cisneros (Random House, 1994).

How the Garcia Girls Lost Their Accents, Julia Alvarez (Algonquin Books of Chapel Hill, 1991).

Hundred Dresses, Eleanor Estes (Harcourt Brace, 1988).

I Capture the Castle, Dodie Smith (Trafalgar Square, 1996).

I Know Why the Caged Bird Sings, Maya Angelou (Fodors Travel, 1996).

The Immense Journey, Loren Eiseley (Random House, 1959).

The Important Book, Margaret W. Brown (HarperCollins Children's Books, 1949).

Incidents in the Life of a Slave Girl, Harriet B. Jacobs (Ayer Co. Publications, 1977).

"In Memory of W. B. Yeats," W. H. Auden, *The Top 500 Poems*, William Harmon (Columbia University Press, 1992).

In the Year of the Boar and Jackie Robinson, Bette B. Lord (HarperCollins Children's Books, 1984).

"Invictus," William E. Henley, *One Hundred and One Classics of Victorian Verse*, Ellen J. Greenfield (Contemporary Books, 1992).

Island of the Blue Dolphins, Scott O'Dell (Dell Publishing Co., 1996).

Jacob Have I Loved, Katherine Paterson (Trophy, 1990).

James and the Giant Peach, Roald Dahl (Disney Press, 1996).

Jane Eyre, Charlotte Brontë (Alfred A. Knopf, 1991).

Jasmine, Bharati Mukherjee (Fawcett Book Group, 1991).

Jason and Marceline, Jerry Spinelli (Little, Brown & Co., 1994).

Jingo Django, Sid Fleischman (Dell Publishing Co., 1995).

The Joy Luck Club, Amy Tan (Ivy Books, 1990).

Julie of the Wolves, Jean C. George (HarperCollins Children's Books, 1995).

The Junkyard Dog, Erika Tamar (Alfred A. Knopf, 1995).

Kane and Abel, Jeffrey Archer (HarperCollins, 1993).

The King James Version of the English Bible, David Daiches (Shoe String Press, 1968).

King of the Wind: The Story of the Godolphin Arabian, Marguerite Henry (S & S Children's, 1990).

The Lais of Marie de France, Marie de France (Penguin Classics, 1986).

Letters from a Slave Girl: The Story of Harriet Jacobs, Mary E. Lyons (Aladdin Paperbacks, 1996).

Letters to a Young Poet, Rainer M. Rilke (Shambhala Publications, 1993).

Life in the Ghetto, Anika D. Thomas (Landmark Editions, 1991).

The Lion, the Witch and the Wardrobe, C. S. Lewis (Dramatic Publishing Co., 1979).

The Little Fishes, Erik Haugaard (Houghton, 1967).

Little House on the Prairie, Laura I. Wilder (HarperCollins Publications, 1990).

Little Women, Louisa M. Alcott (Random House Value Publishing, 1995).

The Little Women Treasury, Carolyn S. Collins (Viking Penguin, 1996).

The Long Loneliness, Dorothy Day (Thomas More, 1989).

Lord of the Flies, William Golding (Viking Penguin, 1997).

Louisa May: The World and Works of Louisa May Alcott, Norma Johnston (Four Winds Press, 1991).

Madeline, Ludwig Bemelmans (Viking Children's Books, 1993).

Maizon at Blue Hill, Jacqueline Woodson (Yearling Books, 1994).

Make Lemonade, Virginia E. Wolff (Point, 1994).

Mama's Girl, Veronica Chambers (Putnam Publishing Group, 1996).

Maniac Magee, Jerry Spinelli (HarperCollins, 1992).

The Man in the Ceiling, Jules Feiffer (HarperCollins Children's Books, 1993).

The Man Who Mistook His Wife for a Hat, Oliver Sacks (Peter Smith Publishing, 1992).

Mary Poppins, P. L. Travers (Dell Publishing Co., 1991).

The Man from the Other Side, Uri Orlev (Puffin Books, 1995).

M. C. Higgins, the Great, Virginia Hamilton (Simon & Schuster, 1991).

Member of the Wedding, Carson McCullers (W. W. Norton & Co., 1988).

The Mennyms, Sylvia Waugh (Camelot, 1996).

The Midwife's Apprentice, Karen Cushman (Clarion Books, 1995).

Misty of Chincoteague, Marguerite Henry (S & S Children's, 1994).

Monster Mama, Liz Rosenberg (Philomel Books, 1993).

Moon Over Crete, Jyotsna Sreenivasan (Holy Cow! Press, 1994).

More English Fairy Tales, Joseph Jacobs (Amereon).

The Mother Child Papers, Alicia Ostriker (Beacon, 1986).

A Mother and Two Daughters, Gail Godwin (Ballantine Books, 1994).

Mother Daughter Revolution: From Good Girls to Great Women, Elizabeth Debold (Bantam Books, 1994).

Mother's Love, Mary Morris (Dell Publishing, 1994).

Mother to Daughter, Daughter to Mother: A Daybook & Reader, edited by Tillie Olsen (Feminist Press at the City University of New York, 1984).

The Mouse and His Child, Russell Hoban (Jordanhill College).

Mrs. Mike, Benedict Freedman (Buccaneer Books, 1981).

The Mystery of Drear House: The Conclusion of the Dies Drear Chronicle, Virginia Hamilton (Aladdin Paperbacks, 1988).

The Nancy Drew series, Carolyn Keene.

Narrative of the Life of Frederick Douglass: An American Slave, Written by Himself, Frederick Douglass (St. Martin's Press, 1993).

A Natural History of the Senses, Diane Ackerman (Random House, 1990).

Needle's Eye, Margaret Drabble (Ivy Books, 1989).

Night, Elie Wiesel (Bantam Books, 1982).

Nina Bonita, Ana M. Machado (Kane/Miller Book Publishing, 1996).

None of the Above, Rosemary Wells (Dial Press, 1974).

The Norton Anthology of African American Literature, Henry L. Gates Jr. (W. W. Norton & Co., 1996).

Notes of a Native Son, James Baldwin (Beacon Press, 1990).

Number the Stars, Lois Lowry (Dell Publishing Co., 1990).

Oh, the Places You'll Go!, Dr. Seuss (Random House, 1990).

Once upon a Time, A. A. Milne (New York Graphics, 1962).

An Outbreak of Peace, Sarah Pirtle (New Society Publishers, 1987).

Owl in Love, Patrice Kindl (Puffin, 1994).

Ozma of Oz, L. Frank Baum (Morrow Junior Books, 1989).

The Perilous Gard, Elizabeth M. Pope (Puffin, 1992).

The Periodic Table, Primo Levi (Random House, 1996).

The Peterkin Papers, Lucretia P. Hale (Thomas Dunne Books, 1994).

Plain City, Virginia Hamilton (Scholastic Trade, 1993).

Poems, Emily Dickinson (Pocket Classics Series, 1995).

Prairie Songs, Pam Conrad (Peter Smith, 1995).

Pride and Prejudice, Jane Austen (Modern Library, 1996).

The Princess and the Goblin, George MacDonald (Airmont, 1967).

The Prophet, Khalil Gibran (Alfred A. Knopf, 1923).

"A Psalm of Life," Henry W. Longfellow, *American Poetry: The Nineteenth Century, Vols. 1 & 2*, John Hollander (The Library of America, 1993).

The Puppy Sister, S. E. Hinton (Delacorte Press, 1995).

Quilting: Poems 1987-1990, Lucille Clifton (BOA Editions, 1991).

Raisin in the Sun, Lorraine Hansbury (Random House, 1995).

Ramona the Pest, Beverly Cleary (Avon Books, 1992).

Rascal, Sterling North (Puffin Books, 1990).

Red Fairy Book, Andrew Lang (Fine Communications, 1994).

The Rime of the Ancient Mariner, Samuel T. Coleridge (Ayer Co. Publications, 1979).

Rising from the Plains, John McPhee (Farrar, Straus & Giroux, 1986).

Rites of Passage: Stories About Growing Up by Black Writers from Around the World, illustrated by Tonya Bolden (Hyperion, 1994).

The Road to Memphis, Mildred D. Taylor (Dial Books for Young Readers, 1990).

Roll of Thunder, Hear My Cry, Mildred D. Taylor (Dial Books for Young Readers, 1976).

The Roman Way, Edith Hamilton (Buccaneer Books, 1994).

A Room of One's Own, Virginia Woolf (Buccaneer Books, 1994).

Ruby, Rosa Guy (Laureleaf, 1992).

Rumors of Peace, Ella Leffland (HarperCollins Publications, 1985).

Running Out of Time, Margaret P. Haddix (S & S Children's Books, 1995).

Sarah Phillips, Andrea Lee (Northeastern University Press, 1993).

Sarah, Plain and Tall, Patricia MacLachlan (HarperCollins Juvenile Books, 1985).

The Secret Garden, Frances H. Burnett (Putnam Publishing Group, 1996).

The Secret of Gumbo Grove, Eleanora E. Tate (Yearling Books, 1996).

Selected Poems, W. H. Auden (Random House, 1979).

Selected Poems, Gwendolyn Brooks (HarperCollins Publications, 1982).

Selected Poems of Emily Dickinson (Random House, 1996).

Selected Poems of Langston Hughes (Alfred A. Knopf, 1959).

The Seven Ravens, Laura Geringer (HarperCrest, 1994).

Shabanu: Daughter of the Wind, Suzanne F. Staples (Random House, 1991).

Shakespeare's Sonnets, comment by Stephen Booth (Yale University Press, 1980).

The Sherwood Ring, Elizabeth M. Pope (Peter Smith Pub., 1989)

The Shimmershine Queens, Camille Yarbrough (Putnam Publishing Group, 1989).

Shimmy Shimmy Shimmy Like My Sister Kate: Looking at the Harlem Renaissance Through Poems, edited by Nikki Giovanni (Henry Holt & Co., 1996).

Shizuko's Daughter, Kyoko Mori (Henry Holt & Co., 1993).

Smoky Night, Eve Bunting (HarBrace Juvenile Books, 1994).

Smoky, the Cow Horse, Will James (Buccaneer Books, 1993).

So Long a Letter, Mariama Ba (Heinemann, 1989).

Sonnets from the Portuguese, Elizabeth B. Browning (Doubleday & Co., 1990).

Sophie's World: A Novel about the History of Philosophy, Jostein Gaarder (Farrar, Straus & Giroux, 1994).

The Souls of Black Folk, W. E. B. Du Bois (Random House, 1996).

Sounder, William Armstrong (HarperCollins Children's Books, 1996).

The Story of Ruby Bridges, Robert Coles (Scholastic, 1995).

Strawberry Girl, Lois Lenski (HarperCollins Children's Books, 1945).

Stuart Little, E. B. White (HarperCollins, 1990).

Sula, Toni Morrisson (Alfred A. Knopf, 1974).

The Sun, the Sea, a Touch of the Wind, Rosa Guy (E. P. Dutton, 1995).

Surely You're Joking Mr. Feynman! Adventures of a Curious Character, Richard Feynman (Bantam Books, 1989).

Susan B. Anthony, Barbara Weisberg (Chelsea House, 1988).

Sweet Valley High series, Francine Pascal (Bantam).

Sweet Whispers, Brother Rush, Virginia Hamilton (Putnam Publishing Group, 1982).

A Tale of Two Cities, Charles Dickens (Random House, 1996).

Taste of Salt: A Story of Modern Haiti, Frances Temple (Trophy, 1994).

Tell Me Again About the Night I Was Born, Jamie L. Curtis (HarperCollins Children's Books, 1996).

Thank You, Dr. Martin Luther King, Eleanora E. Tate (Skylark, 1996).

Their Eyes Were Watching God, Zora N. Hurston (HarperCollins, 1990).

There's a Boy in the Girls' Bathroom, Louis Sachar (Random House, 1994).

The Thorn Birds, Colleen McCullough (Avon Books, 1978).

A Thousand Acres, Jane Smiley (Fawcett Book Group, 1992).

A Thousand Pieces of Gold, Ruthanne L. McCunn (Beacon Press, 1989).

Time Cat: The Remarkable Journeys of Jason and Gareth, Lloyd Alexander (Puffin, 1996).

To Kill a Mockingbird, Harper Lee (HarperCollins, 1995).

Toning the Sweep, Angela Johnson (Point, 1994).

A Tree Grows in Brooklyn, Betty Smith (G. K. Hall & Co., 1993).

The Trials of Molly Sheldon, Julian F. Thompson (Henry Holt & Co., 1995).

Tuck Everlasting, Natalie Babbit (Farrar, Straus & Giroux, 1986).

Twelfth Night, William Shakespeare (Random House Value Publishing, 1994).

The Twenty-One Balloons, William P. Du Bois (Puffin Books, 1986).

Twenty Years at Hull-House, Jane Addams (University of Illinois Press, 1990).

Understood Betsy, Dorothy Canfield (Amereon, 1976).

Up a Road Slowly, Irene Hunt (Silver Burdett, 1993).

Up the Down Staircase, Bel Kaufman (HarperCollins, 1991).

Value Tale series, Spencer Johnson and Ann D. Johnson (Goldencraft).

Venus Among the Fishers, Scott O'Dell (Houghton Mifflin Co., 1995).

Walk Two Moons, Sharon Creech (McClelland & Stewart, 1995).

Weetzie Bat, Francesca L. Block (HarperCollins Children's Books, 1989).

We Were the Mulvaneys, Joyce C. Oates (NAL/Dutton, 1996).

What's Happening to Me?, Peter Mayle (Lyle Stuart, 1986).

When Hitler Stole Pink Rabbit, Judith Kerr (Bantam Doubleday Dell Books for Young Readers, 1987).

When I Was Little: A Four-Year-Old's Memoir of Her Youth, Jamie L. Curtis (Trophy, 1994).

When the Nightingale Sings, Joyce C. Thomas (Harpercrest, 1992).

Where Did I Come From?, Peter Mayle (Lyle Stuart, 1986)

Where the Lilies Bloom, Vera Cleaver and Bill Cleaver (Dramatic Publishing Co., 1977).

Wilma Rudolph, Tom Biracree (Holloway House Publishing Co., 1991).

The Wind in the Willows, Kenneth Grahame (St. Martin's Press, 1995).

Winnie the Pooh, A. A. Milne (Dutton Children's Books, 1992).

Winter on the Farm, Laura I. Wilder (HarperCollins, 1996).

Wise Child, Monica Furlong (Random House, 1989).

The Witch of Blackbird Pond, Elizabeth G. Speare (Laureleaf, 1993).

A Wizard of Earthsea, Ursula K. Le Guin (Bantam Books, 1984).

The Wizard of Oz series, L. Frank Baum.

The Wolves of Willoughby Chase, Joan Aiken (Bantam Doubleday Dell Books for Young Readers, 1987).

Women's Friendships: A Collection of Short Stories, edited by Susan Koppelman (University of Oklahoma Press, 1991).

Women Who Run with the Wolves: Myths and Stories of the Wild Women Archetype, Clarissa P. Estes (Ballantine, 1992).

Words by Heart, Ouida Sebestyen (Little, Brown & Co., 1979).

The World of Little House, Christina W. Eriksson and Carolyn S. Collins (HarperCollins Juvenile Books, 1996).

A Wrinkle in Time, Madeleine L'Engle (Farrar, Straus & Giroux, 1962).

Wuthering Heights, Emily Brontë (Scribners Reference, 1996).

The Yearling, Marjorie K. Rawlings (S & S Children's Books, 1992).

Yolanda's Genius, Carol Fenner (Macmillan Publishing, 1997).

The Youngest Science: Notes of a Medicine Watcher, Lewis Thomas (Viking Penguin, 1995).

Zeely, Virginia Hamilton (Aladdin, 1993).

Zlateh the Goat and Other Stories, Isaac B. Singer (HarperCollins Children's Book, 1966).

ACKNOWLEDGMENTS

I am especially grateful to the following people, without whom this book would not have been possible:

My mother, Charlotta, for instilling in me an appreciation of reading; and to my grandmother who showed me the value of women's clubs; my stepmother, Felice, and father, Buddy, for their love and support; Belinda Caraballo, for two wonderful weeks of morning walks and conversation that led to the idea for the mother-daughter book club; all the mothers and daughters in the book club for allowing me to share our collective journey; Pam Sacks, for her willingness to help shape the club and for sharing her in-depth knowledge of books with us—your book recommendations were perfect; Lisa, for her faith in this book and for being a rock and a refuge during every phase of the project; and the entire staff at Seth Godin Productions, particularly Robin and Sarah, for all their hard work; my editor at HarperCollins, Megan Newman, for her nudging, her enthusiasm and her most constructive criticism, and to the wonderful team she put together that helped make this book possible; Teresa, for her creative energy and ability to insightfully give my thoughts and experiences a resting place on these pages; and to Teresa's family for sharing so much of her with me; Jan Verhage, Executive Director, Girl Scout Council of The Nation's Capital, for being such a ready, willing and able flow of information, advice and encouragement.

Thanks also to my friend and colleague, Deborah Willis, for allowing me—as she always so graciously does—continual access to her awesome knowledge bank and fine sensibilities. And to the staff at the Center for African American History and Culture: Steven C. Newsome, Toni Brady, Deirdre Cross, Elanna Haywood and Mark Wright who provided understanding and support. I am indebted to Barbara Blum and my fellow board members at the Adams National Bank, for believing I could do this; and to my best friend Joanne Williams, for being a sounding board and counsel on every leg of my journey with this book.

Special thanks to all the African-American writers who have provided through their work the inspiration that shapes many of the club's discussions. And finally, a warm heartfelt thank-you to the many people who responded to my request for help on the book by contributing a book list or an interview, recommending a resource or just lending an ear. I'll never be able to thank you enough.

—Shireen Dodson, January 1997

For their contributions of time, thought and inspiration, I extend my thanks to the following people:

To my mother, Maxine, and my father, George, who created in our family life a haven for creative thought and for reading, writing, exploring and sharing ideas; my sister Susan, a busy designer and mother of two daughters, who really didn't have time, but made time anyway, to bring her talents to the book; Beth, who forwarded the publishers my way; to Leslie, for allowing me to learn from her experience; to our goodhearted staff at Readmore Communications, particularly to Karen, for her research and organization; to Lisa, Robin, Julie and Sarah for introducing me to Shireen and this special opportunity, and for their work.

To Shireen, for starting her Mother-Daughter Book Club, for asking me to help her share the idea with others, and for bringing candor and good humor to our partnership; to Shireen's husband, Leroy, and my Steve, for their technical assistance at all hours of day and night; and to all the mothers and daughters in Shireen's club as well as my own—Hannah and Anne Clark, Hannah, Rebecca and Wendy Hartz, Sierra and Donna Patterson, Stephanie and Helen Shum, Kate and Jamie Sullivan, Lynae and Darlene Turner and Stephanie and Karen Wesolowski—for sharing their thoughts and ideas; Elizabeth Debold and her coauthors, for the inspiration that came of reading their *Mother*

Daughter Revolution: From Good Girls to Great Women, and to the other generous contributors who spoke so enthusiastically in our interviews—Susan Bailey, Nina Baym, Carolyn Collins, Martha Decherd, Bonnie Diamond, Sumru Erkut, Rosa Guy, Virginia Hamilton, Alice Letvin, Ann Martin, Harriet Mosatche, Connie Porter, Whitney Ransome, Pam Sacks, Ellen Silber, Joan Franklin Smutny, Lee Temkin, Bertha Waters and Elizabeth Wheeler; to all my friends who came or called—or refrained from both—at all the right times, whose experience and enthusiasm are an ongoing theme in my life.

And finally, to my own treasure of a family—Steve, Rachel, Rebecca and Aaron—each one of whom accommodated this project in so many ways every day, through birthdays and holidays, nights and weekends; my younger sister Holly, with whom I have shared books and book talk from the beginning; to Steve's cousin Martha, a gifted media library teacher who has helped build our family library and our interest in the widest world of authors and stories; and to Steve's mom, Dolly, with whom I have shared books and thoughts about them for twelve happy years. The important thing about appreciation is to truly feel it. I do.

—Teresa Barker, January 1997

INDEX

W

ABOUT THE AUTHOR

Shireen Dodson is the Assistant Director
Smithsonian Institution's Center for African American
and Culture. She serves on the Board of Directors of th
National Bank, the District of Columbia Chamber of C
and the Girl Scout Council of the Nation's Capital. She is
member of the Washington Chapter of Jack and Jill of .
Inc., and was a founding member of the Coalition of 1
Women of DC, Inc. She and her husband, Leroy M. Fyke
Northwest Washington, D.C., with their three children, I
sixteen, Morgan, eleven, and Skylar, six.

ABOUT THE WRITER

Teresa Barker is a writer, editor and communicati
sultant. She has written extensively about issues related t
culture, education and health. Her work has appearec
Chicago Tribune, the *Chicago Sun-Times*, the *Eugene Regist*
the *Nashville Tennessean* and in other newspapers, magazi
nationally syndicated publications. She is vice president
ative director of Readmore Communications in Chicag
she founded with her husband, Steve Weiner. They live in
Grove, Illinois, with their three children, Rachel, nine, F
six, and Aaron, eleven.

DESIGN NOTES

This book was designed by Susan Barker Brown a
Brown & Associates in Portland, Oregon. Typographer
Brem produced the text.

THE MOTHER-DAUGHTER BOOK CLUBS OF AMERICA NEWS

If you enjoy your mother-daughter book club and want to share your experiences with girls and moms across the country, subscribe today. You will receive a bimonthly newsletter filled with Mother-Daughter Book Club news and views. Plus author profiles, book reviews by girls and moms, suggested book-related club activities and much, much more.

Like the Mother-Daughter Book Club, the newsletter promotes a love of reading and inspires communication and sharing between mothers and daughters.

Edited by Shireen Dodson.

To order, simply mail in the card below:

The Mother-Daughter Book Clubs of America, Inc.
6100 13th Street NW
Washington, DC 20011
E-mail: SLDodson@erols.com

_____

Name

_____

Address

_____

City   State   Zip

1 year (6 bimonthly issues) for $14.95
PAYMENT ENCLOSED
(Orders subject to acceptance.)

About the Author

Shireen Dodson is the Assistant Director for the Smithsonian Institution's Center for African American History and Culture. She serves on the Board of Directors of the Adams National Bank, the District of Columbia Chamber of Commerce and the Girl Scout Council of the Nation's Capital. She is an active member of the Washington Chapter of Jack and Jill of America, Inc., and was a founding member of the Coalition of 100 Black Women of DC, Inc. She and her husband, Leroy M. Fykes, live in Northwest Washington, D.C., with their three children, Leroy III, sixteen, Morgan, eleven, and Skylar, six.

About the Writer

Teresa Barker is a writer, editor and communications consultant. She has written extensively about issues related to family, culture, education and health. Her work has appeared in the *Chicago Tribune*, the *Chicago Sun-Times*, the *Eugene Register-Guard*, the *Nashville Tennessean* and in other newspapers, magazines and nationally syndicated publications. She is vice president and creative director of Readmore Communications in Chicago, which she founded with her husband, Steve Weiner. They live in Buffalo Grove, Illinois, with their three children, Rachel, nine, Rebecca, six, and Aaron, eleven.

Design Notes

This book was designed by Susan Barker Brown at Susan Brown & Associates in Portland, Oregon. Typographer Denise Brem produced the text.